"Immigration, immigration, immigration!"

David Cann

Political Intelligence Publications

The definition of an 'immigrant' is an internationally recognised term - and refers to anyone who moves to another country for at least a year.

"Immigration, immigration, immigration" – is all that seems to be dominating the TV schedules and news in the run-up to the 2015 General Election.

Though for those living among it all and experiencing the detrimental effects and impact mass immigration is having on their lives, villages, towns and cities, it is an omnipresent topic of debate that many others – Pro-EU have long preferred to ignore and instead keep swept under the carpet.

Often branding anyone who points out; "…there's simply too many "people" entering the country," – as being xenophobic racists - and coming-up with derisory justifications, such as 'immigrants' bring so much more to the table and adding to the wondrous diversity of what multiculturalism can offer.

In many respects this can be true and why you'll probably find the largest number of people from a whole variety of ethnic backgrounds already living here in the UK, than perhaps any other country in the world and especially since the country joined the European Union in 1973, - not forgetting the Windrush voyage from the Caribbean to Tilbury docks back in 1948.

"Today's" debate about immigration was also a cause of concern back in those days, but times were different then. In 1948, Britain was just beginning to recover from the ravages of war. There was plenty of work, but the Caribbean's first clashed with the indigenous working classes over the issue of accommodation.

Like in 1960's when faced with mounting tension over lack of housing and high immigration; Peter Griffiths, Conservative MP for Smethwick, the Conservative local council decided it would buy-up any properties that came onto the market and let them only to white families.

This occurrence in Smethwick was shown on the 15 March 2015, Channel 4, when they aired "Britain's Racist Election" - another timely exploration, (further on we look into other TV programmes recently shown and covering the subject of immigration) - of how an anti-immigration campaign in the 1964 General Election tore a community apart and triggered what has been claimed as one of the worst chapters in British race relations.

So serious were its implications for race relations, it resulted in a visit from the American civil rights activist, Malcolm X, just nine days before he was assassinated in New York.

But it was still something that could have changed the face of Britain forever, had the Labour government not stepped in and quashed the council's plans and policy.

Today, Marshall Street is home to hundreds of people from all cultures. An official blue plaque, commemorating the visit of Malcolm X, is high on the wall of the end house, at the junction with West Park Road.

And it's true, there were some ignorant racist people placing signs in their window; "No Blacks, No Dogs, No Irish," - putting the Irish at the bottom of the list due to the "troubles" in Ireland and the bombings taking place on the mainland of the UK by the IRA.

Places like Smethwick attracted workers from the West Indies and Indian sub-continent.

They came for exactly the same reason that Welsh immigrants arrived during the previous century, and French Huguenots before them.

The factories and foundries were booming and there was always work for people who were prepared to put in long hours for low pay.

As a result, Black and Asian workers did more work for less pay than their white counterparts.

Following WWII, London was badly bombed and bombsites remained until the mid-60s in some areas such as Bethnal Green, Poplar, Docklands and

Hackney, East London and other parts of London, such as Old Kent Road, Brixton, Herne Hill and Clapham - and the rest of the city and country in general.

You have to appreciate, that black people were as alien to the white population as they were to them. It must be said in the early days they were excluded from much of the social and economic life around them, though they began to adjust along with the institutions they brought with them; the churches, and a co-operative method of saving called the 'Pardner' system.

At the same time, Caribbeans began to participate in organisations to which they did have access: trade unions, local councils and professional and staff associations.   It was mainly London Transport, British Rail and the Post Office that employed the vast majority of them.

Again, the same old excuse was bantered about back then that "lazy British workers" didn't want to do those jobs and why "immigrants" were only filling a gap in the market. This was far from true and was more to do with the unions demanding better conditions and higher pay.

Like Labours' recent 'open-door' policy, they did the same in the 1950's and advertised jobs in Africa and the West Indies so as to set a cat among the pigeons of the British workers and their unions.

However, that's history and more important the black population began to assimilate and in time the majority of white people accepted them, as did black folk begin to trust their white counterparts.

Most working class kids from inner city boroughs during the 1960's onwards grew-up with black folks, then the Asians and particularly after Idi Amin expelled thousands of them from Uganda in 1972.

According to Mike Philips on the BBCs programme; Windrush - the Passengers; "It was also by the start of the seventies, West-Indians were a familiar and established part of the British population. One indication of their influence and effect on British life and culture is the Notting Hill Carnival.

Throughout the seventies, the children of the first wave of post-war Caribbean migrants began to develop their own 'black culture' which is now part of a black British style shared by Africans, Asians and white young people alike.

The people of the Windrush, their children and grandchildren have all played a role in creating a new concept of what it means to be "British."

To be British in the present day implies a person who might have their origins in Africa, the Caribbean, China, India, Greece, Turkey or anywhere else in the spectrum of nations that once had connections to the British Empire or Commonwealth.

The British national self-image has been thoroughly remodeled in a very short time. Seen against the deadly agonies associated with ethnic conflicts in other European countries, Britain offers the example of a nation, which can live comfortably with a new and inclusive concept of citizenship."

If anything, this is testament to how open minded, fair and warm hearted the majority of the British public were and still are for this to have worked and be the success story that it is today.

Many white English/British folk are proud that black and white have been able to unite, because they too appreciate what other cultures can contribute to the country.

Perhaps it could be claimed this hasn't so much been the case with the Asian communities, and probably something to do with the divide and differences of their religions; whereas the vast majority of Black immigrants were/are Christians.

As mentioned, many of the "English/British" also come from "immigrant" families, including the Welsh, the French Huguenots and Anglo-Saxons to name just a few.

(The names "Wales" and "Welsh" are traced to the Proto-Germanic word "Walhaz"; meaning "foreigner", "stranger", "Roman", "Romance-speaker" or "Celtic-speaker" which was used by the ancient Germanic peoples to describe inhabitants of the former Roman Empire, who were largely romanised and spoke Latin or Celtic languages.)

Though as said and, to be fair, times have changed and moved on since this era, that curiously enough it's not just members of the indigenous white population who are up in arms about the "recent" increase in mass immigration into the UK.

For you will find many descendants of the Windrush generation, along with those Asian families who first arrived here in the 1960s and 1970s - also vehemently objecting to the ever increasing volume of immigrants flooding the country's villages, town and cities, as this is a matter that effects everyone.

This is why it has nothing to do with - "where you come from," – but all to do with excessive unstoppable numbers of people continuously entering the country.

December 2014 - Speaking to the Sunday Times about Immigration and the BBC, John Humphrys, Presenter of BBC Radio 4's Today Programme, said;

"We didn't interrogate immigration rigorously enough."

"We failed to look at what our job was."

"We were too institutionally nervous of saying, isn't immigration getting a little bit out of hand?

And, can we be critical of multiculturalism?"

It is vitally important to understand that those opposing the mass-immigration the country is currently undergoing and the UKs membership of the EU, has nothing to do with pitting one brother against another, xenophobia, intolerance or racism - and all to do with the math = "numbers", - nothing more, nothing less.

You have to be able to grasp that the 1%, whom we touch on in other chapters and who are a larger number than many appreciate - approximately 73 million out of a world population of 7,301,925,777 billion as on 17 March 2015; couldn't care less if a two headed, black, yellow, white or green one eyed monster did all the work whilst making and saving them loads of money in the same process. Who does the work is totally irrelevant to them, as long as it all gets done is all that matters.

The only person/s who are affected by "someone else" doing this work; is the person/s who were first in line to do it.

The "divide and rule" strategy has long been used by the 1%. If it's not religion, then it's colour or race.

Without sounding too impertinent, it's a sad fact and not really the fault of the masses, but many are totally ignorant in their 'world view' due to being badly educated – which is another tool in the box of tricks the 1% have long used against them, that being "poor" as well - means they're not so well travelled either.

By creating and having a badly educated flock around them makes it easier to manipulate and control them. If only they knew how happy they made the 1% when they refuse to vote, - it would probably change their attitude and they'd vote more often.

It is this not being so well educated, the working-class (approximately five/six billion worldwide) and not being in the same position as the middle-classes (approximately one/two billion worldwide) or the 1% that prevents them being able to travel the world and get to know other people, - their races and cultures - that unfortunately tends to make them that somewhat more ignorant and inexperienced - than perhaps someone better educated. And we're not talking about your package-holidays to Benidorm or similar places which were/are typically for a week or two in the sun. As the majority drink high volumes of alcohol throughout their duration and hardly make it further than the hotel swimming pool.

We're talking about "culture", the arts, learning languages and conversing in in-depth conversations with their hosts and when a connection and understanding is often experienced as a result.

Of course times have changed from the 60s and 70s and many people travel further afield and why things are nowhere as bad as they were for previous generations. Yet the majority of the working classes have been deliberately and subliminally attuned to consent to 'their lot' – that most appear happy enough to do, for as some say; - 'ignorance is bliss.'

However, ignorance leads to narrow mindedness and without even knowing it they naturally become almost blinkered with their outlook to life in general.

Often becoming one of those people who would say; "You'd never get me eating any of that foreign muck…" and probably picked up such an outlook and attitude to life due to a parent/s or someone else close to their upbringing.

How tragic it is that these types of people have been denied such experiences, thus indirectly denying themselves the wonders and delights the world can offer and not even be aware that they are ultimately the loser by being deprived this way.

Racism has been with us ever since man came down from the trees and first took to caves to dwell in. Racism is experienced within countries of the "same colour"; as there are many African's, say Nigerians, and of course not them all, whose views towards Jamaicans are extremely derogatory.

Slavery was already in existence and something the Whiteman came across in Africa whilst on his travels to conquer the world - and being solely materialistic in their aims and objectives; whilst wanting to enforce their own belief system on whoever they encountered, paid and played the same game, making a huge and "legitimate" business model out of it.

Egypt and the Roman Empire long had slaves. Many places in Asia and Africa, today still have them, despite it being "technically" illegal.

The "working-classes" of the world, in excess of five billion, that despite not being shackled, the way many of them are treated and accept it as so, with countless of people living in abject poverty and for centuries at that, then you could arguably say "slavery" still exists and on every continent of the world.

Because of previous wars; there are many Irish and Scottish folk who today in 2015 irrationally despise the English, and vice-versa. This type of nonsensical hatred and racism goes on all around the globe with religion being the major cause for these illogical feelings people hold against one another. People they have never even met or likely ever to do so, yet can still hold this abhorrence towards them.

Generally, racism consists of both prejudice and discrimination that is often based on social preconceptions of biological differences between people, such as the colour of someone's skin or what "God" they may believe in.

It often takes the form of social actions, practices or beliefs, or political systems that consider different "races" to be ranked as inherently superior or inferior to each other, based on presumed shared inheritable traits, abilities, or qualities.

It may also hold that members of different races should be treated differently – though mainly because of "historic" events and happenings.

So bearing all this in mind; - of course racism exists and perhaps it always will do whilst such fundamental differences subsist in such a divisive world.

In some respects it could be argued that's what the whole conception of the "Common Market" was all about, to help overcome these barriers and vanquish these indifferences.

Yet research and further understanding as to who was really behind the foundations of such a virtuous notion and discussed further on - soon dispels this myth.

As already stated; today's arguments against membership of the EU has nothing to do with nationalism, discrimination or racism - and all to do with the math = "numbers."

Those with no real argument or reason often attack those wishing to explain what the Treaty of Rome/Lisbon/Maastricht really means.

Take the case of Mr Farage, he has been regularly criticised for making unsubstantiated "ludicrous" claims, when he has implied "millions" of Romanian's could now come to live and work the UK.

Though technically speaking he is 100% right, as under the Treaty of Rome 'Free Movement of Labour' clause - Articles (48 to 73), any person from any EU member state can enter the UK to live and "work", just like anyone from the UK can go to any country within the EU and do the same.

The main reason Romanians or Bulgarians appear to be singled-out, is because they were the last countries to recently join the EU in 2014 and as the following figures confirm they have begun their gradual move over to the UK.

In the time since Great Britain first joined the EU in 1973; Migrationwatch-UK have proven that millions have been free to enter the UK and millions have, though not as many millions have emigrated from the country.

You have to be conscious of the fact that the governments Office for National Statistics (ONS) figures, quite often do not truly reflect the real number of immigrants living the UK.

Many 'illegal' ones have smuggled themselves in; you only have to witness the daily running of the gauntlet that takes place at border-crossings such as Calais in France to fully comprehend this.

There are yet other countries who too wish to join the EU. Albania is being primed to do just that and with the backing of the EU.

According to an Associated Press report 13 February 2015: Tens of thousands of immigrants mostly Kosovo Albanians, but also Syrians, Afghans, Iraqis and others have passed through Serbia and into European Union member Hungary, a gateway into the 28-nation bloc and whose ultimate goal is to end up in countries such as the UK.

Hungarian Prime Minister Viktor Orban, said his country needs new, tougher rules allowing for the detention and expulsion of illegal migrants, otherwise Hungary would "turn into a refugee camp."

They began to experience a tide of Kosovars shortly after the EU sponsored a 2014 free-travel agreement that allowed Kosovars to travel freely into Serbia.

Officials in Kosovo estimate at least 100,000 Kosovars have emigrated since August 2014.

Hungarian authorities say, about 23,200 migrants already have been detained in Hungary this year 2015, compared to 43,000 in all of 2014 and just 2,157 in 2013.

 Once migrants reach Hungary, many travel to richer members throughout Europe.

On the 18 February 2015 the BBC reported that in January 2014, the number of Romanians and

Bulgarians "working" in the UK has risen by 15% year-on-year, Office for National Statistics (ONS) figures show.

Within the last three months alone - of 2014, there were 172,000 people working in the UK who had been born in either one of those eastern European countries.

The figures also show that the total number of EU workers in the UK rose by 200,000 - or 10.5% - to almost 1.9 million.

The BBC showed a film report of hundreds of illegal immigrants who had travelled five continents trying to smuggle themselves into Europe and were being held-up in France; as yet again the majority were destined for the UK.

Out of those interviewed they admitted and will tell you this time and again; it's Great Britain they want to settle in.

It seems whenever an individual, interest group or political party makes the observation and speaks out that there are simply too many people in any one particular location or area and no matter whatever their race, creed or colour - and where it becomes almost impossible to get a job or find a home with affordable rent, a school for their children to attend or the hospital treatment they need;

that if they dare have the affront to voice their opinions and wish to complain - there is this sector of society - including the mainstream media - who soon steps-in and comes-down on them like a ton of bricks.

Often branding the observer as being a racist, when that's really not the case.

The time has come for these false allegations and weak kind of arguments to be confronted, debated and addressed whenever they arise.

For its this constant denial and sweeping under the carpet of the true facts and figures that will indeed create umbrage amongst those trying to reveal the truth and highlight the seriousness of this problem and their own situations.

As a collective, it is as damaging to all sides, as who really wants to live in an area or country where there's no job security, no school places and with dentist surgeries and GPs needing up to two-weeks or more before they can even see a patient.

That house prices and rents are so high, that without state benefits or Universal Credits, average people simply cannot afford to rent or buy.

According to an article in the Independent newspaper, 19 February 2013, more than 1,700 people applied for just eight jobs at a new coffee shop, in an indication as to how many people are desperate to find employment.

Coffee shop chain Costa, said it received 1,701 applications for the posts at their new branch in

Mapperley, Nottingham.

The situation got worse, when it was reported just over a year later on the 24 March 2014, thousands of job hunters queued for hours in a bid to get one of just forty jobs on offer at the Aldi budget supermarket chain.

According to the Huffington Post; 'A mother-of-two who had queued since 10am was reported saying that it;' "…looked more like auditions for X-Factor, not a job for Aldi."

Aldi area manager Leon Donald, said: "A previous event similar to this attracted around 1,500 people so we knew this event would be well-attended."

THE SAME CAKE

"Workers", like slaves, are required to help keep the 1%, at the top.   It's big business. The conglomerates and banks need droves upon droves of workers to keep their profits high - whilst keeping wages as low possible.

Every now and again the workers, sensing they are again getting a raw deal, rebel. If not already existing, trade-unions are sometimes formed and insist on improved conditions and fairer take-home pay. At times a compromise is reached - and until the next time.

Even though in many respects, free markets and capitalism is a good thing; due to its current nonsensical set-up, is why quite often many businesses fail or go under.

Private businesses are constantly striving for profits, they typically rely on investors and boards of directors who all want a slice of the cake – annually!

This means year in, year out, and no matter how large or small these companies are, banks included, they all pay out a dividend, if of course they can.

Though that's the real problem as most do make a profit, huge profits at that, yet time and again they take out far too much and not leave enough in the company accounts for continuous reinvestment or a rainy day.

So it's a bit like a dog forever chasing its own tail, and perhaps why companies such as Woolworth eventually demise.

However, we digress, so because "big business" relies on generating profits and beyond all else, it means they are always wanting to "save" money. Normally it's their labour/workforce that costs the most.

We all know that if there is a shortage of anything, whether it be a commodity, resource or labour, then the market price will reflect this. Too much or little demand will determine the value, which means it will rise or fall and like what's recently happened to the price of oil.

The same applies to wages, since the world

recession/s wages have been stagnant for some years now.

Apart from the billions of pounds lost each year in corporate tax avoidance and evasion schemes, that again involves most of the major banks and with full knowledge of our MPs:

When you have a country with a population well in excess of 63,000,000 like that of the UK, with well over 30 million plus working and 1.91 million unemployed and on benefits; the generated income from the workforce's tax and contributions will pay towards keeping those unemployed fed, clothed and housed.

This system can work quite well as there's an abundance of wealth and income that actually goes into the government coffers that should allow a rich nation such as the UK to be able to maintain the forever changing numbers of unemployed and sick people as and when they arise.

Nevertheless, due to present and past governments and their continuous incompetence, stealing, wasting, mismanaging and sheer negligence of the billions (trillions in the long term) of pounds that goes through the treasury and out of the public purse, is the true reason as to why so many are forever kept at the starting blocks of life and awaiting for the starting gun to be fired.

This continuously raping and pillaging of public funds keeps them forever needing to replace the church roof.

Thus the shortage of these funds - despite all this generated money, the country is constantly in debt - and even more so now than perhaps at any other time in its history.

So, knowing all this, living and going through it generation after generation, experiencing the lack of services, social housing, schools, hospitals, old people's homes etc. - then how on earth can you then expect to allow so many others to flood into the country and in many cases completely taking over certain areas?

And who too now all need feeding from the same cake, when it's not as if the cake has gotten any bigger.

In fact it's obviously reduced in its original size, but the amount of mouths expected to be fed from this very same cake has grown beyond all reasonably expectations.

That it is due to this and this alone that is causing the upsurge and growing support of the right-wing parties in general – for other political party's - particularly Labour, have since totally ruined the cake.

It's often misguidedly claimed that those in opposition of the European Union are right wing xenophobic extremist, and that in some, or many cases - this is true.

Yet there's a real irony here, for as you'll see further on; the key players and draftsmen of the Treaty of Rome, are exposed in the book; "The Nazi Roots of the Brussels EU", that the founding president Walter Hallstein, was by no means the only architect working on the legalities of the Treaty, that he, among others, were also key players in Adolf Hitler's Nazi regime.

Previously, typically the disquiet about the treaties of Rome, Lisbon or Maastricht, often came from the far right and middle-right conservative type of interest groups and political parties.

Now, it's coming from anyone wise enough to know what the clauses within the treaties actual mean, and by those whose lives have been turned upside down or even devastated due to them.

How times have changed and in less than 50 years with Margaret Thatcher decimating the coal miner's union, the likes of Eddie Shah doing the same to industries such as the print and then with the government's privatisation of the oil, gas, electric, water and railway industries and with the unions no longer holding much sway, along with the country joining the EU - is the real reason why within the UK and Europe in general the exploitation of workers is on the increase and why zero hour contracts are all the rage and why wages have remained low and for so long.

Perhaps, it's true 'the print' needed to adjust and modernise due to technology and new ways of printing.

Though the same can't be said of the coal industry; to close it down in the way "Tories" did, completely destroyed parts of the country, so much so these "Labour" voting regions have never recovered from it. Ruining generations of great men, proud people and tight-knit communities.

Considering all the controversy over "Fracking" and that smokeless coal fuel has long existed, it's not entirely true British coal mining couldn't compete with the rest of the world, for it could have, especially if the right investment had been injected into it.

It was more to do with annihilating the coal miner's union, "destroy them" - 'the hardest of the bunch' - and the rest will scatter like skittles.

In 2012, the Russian Government approved a long-term programme for the development of the coal industry for the period up to 2030. Russia are the sixth largest coal producer after China, the US,

India, Australia and Indonesia.

The Labour party, especially since Tony Blair's influence over the party, his involvement in the Iraq war, their obvious betrayal of the "common man" and the trade unions, is why they have completely lost their way and original purpose.

Which was too stand-up-for and defend the working-classes.

In their process of modernisation they seem to have totally forgotten or ignored their original objectives and what gave them the vote in the first place.

Yet Labour have long known this and perhaps out of all the political parties they have been the most deceptive. So deep is their deception to the indigenous workers, it could be said its tantamount to treason.

For as mentioned elsewhere, they have long gone seeking a more subservient worker from outside the country.

This is because they know they have failed the British working-class so miserably, they have had to rely on the "immigrant vote" instead. This means in order to gain power, they had to flood the country with as many as they could.

The Liberals like to see themselves as middle of the road; rights for all, and rightly so. Yet like Labour, especially following Nick Glegg's U-turn on tuition fees and being part of a coalition government, they too have completely lost their sense of direction.

Instead of concentrating on their own purpose and obligations at home, they appear more worried about Britain's membership of the EU and making sure they remain in it.

In addition, it's these very same three political parties that led the British public blindly into the Common Market, as it was once called back then when the UK first joined the EU.

Collectively, each and every consecutive government had chosen to deliberately ignore all its failings and the warning-signs that something significantly was and still is going wrong within Europe and, even more so within their own country.

Yet, they still aren't prepared to admit to this or alter their stance on the situation.

How none of these political parties couldn't see that the huge numbers of additional immigrants, both legal and illegal saturating the country and in some cases completely deluging a particular area, and not identifying the problem as to why there's not enough social housing, jobs, schools or healthcare and that the welfare bill is so astronomically high, - is completely beyond all comprehension.

And that's why it's a deliberate deceptive act that has nothing to do with incomprehension, incompetence or not seeing what's going on around them.

Your average MP is middleclass, and in many cases they are millionaires. Even if they are in opposition, including expenses, their income is tenfold the national average.

Many would rather employ a migrant worker, as there's often less wages to pay.

They have a second or third home and typically in a member state in Europe and why it's in "their" interest the UK remains in the EU and the flooding of immigrants into the country continues.

ACT OF TREASON

22 February 2011, the true legacy of the Labour government was exposed in a comprehensive review by the think-tank Migration Watch UK.

The study comes as an independent poll revealed three in four Britons believe immigration is a big problem with major concerns, especially growing among younger people who are facing record levels of unemployment and little prospects for their futures, that many see nothing else but low paid dead-end jobs or a life on benefits.

As the report also revealed three in every four new jobs created since 1997 have been accounted for by immigrant workers, – that's a staggering 75%.

One in four children was born to a foreign mother = 25%.

A third of future extra households will be due to immigration = 33.5%.

500,000 extra foreign-born children arrived at a primary school.

Official figures show up to 5,500,000 non-UK born people arrived in the country as long term immigrants between 1997 and 2010 – the equivalent of almost one every minute.

Around 2,300,000 left over the same period meaning the UK population increased by around 3,200,000 as a direct result of foreign migrants.

Some 80% of those also came from outside the EU, most migrants came from the Indian Sub-Continent, Africa and the Middle East, and not taking into account the many Chinese and other far eastern Asians who appear to be going under the radar, yet whose businesses and property developments are cropping up all over the country.

The above figures speak for themselves, that ever since the ratification of the Treaty of Rome; Free Movement of Labour, under European Law, no one technically even requires a passport to travel within member states of the EU.

This is why many people can enter the UK with the most basic of identification, such as a European driving licence or Citizen ID card.

That in turn has made it so much easier for those living outside the EU to also gain entry using the most simplest of fraudulent documentation.

1 February 2014, the Telegraph newspaper disclosed that thousands of migrants have attempted to claim British benefits by using fake documents, entering into false marriages, and lying about being related to European citizens in order to gain access into the UK.

Minister's knew of this, but deceptively chose to hide the evidence that migrants were abusing EU rules and defrauding the British benefits system as MPs on all sides of the house debated the Immigration Bill.

You really couldn't make this up; but the BBC reported on the 17 March 2015, that illegal immigrants are being smuggled 'out' of the UK via Dover, so as to evade deportation, then smuggled back 'in.'

An undercover BBC journalist filmed 21 illegal immigrants inside a lorry being taken on to a ferry and into France. Most said they intended to return.

John Vine, former Independent Chief Inspector of Borders and Immigration, said "...the film exposed serious issues."

Illegal immigrants leave the UK to evade deportation by the authorities in the UK, but some are then being smuggled back in to the UK after being registered as "asylum seekers" in Italy.

An asylum loophole means that, if they are then caught in the UK, they are likely to be returned to Italy rather than their country of origin.

If it wasn't for UKIP, then the question of immigration wouldn't even have been on the 2015 General Election agenda, and perhaps shows the electorate the importance of such a party being in existence.

According to a study by Migrationwatch-UK, titled; "Immigration – Labour's enduring legacy to Britain", it reports that the scale of immigration movement is the largest seen in the UK since the Saxons invaded more than 1,000 years ago.

The research by leading demographer, Professor David Coleman of Oxford University, concluded that if immigration continues at its present level the 'white British' may become a minority in the UK by the late 2060s.

In the inner parts of some city areas such as London, Leicester, Bradford or Birmingham – this is already virtually the case.

According to Sir Andrew Green, chairman of Migrationwatch-UK: "In the years to come immigration will be seen as Labour's great betrayal. The sheer scale of what has occurred is changing Britain fundamentally and irrevocably and in ways the majority of the population did not ask for, were not consulted about and did not wish to see."

He continues: "When you consider that three million extra people on this island equates to the creation of three cities the size of Birmingham, seven the size of Manchester or twenty the size of Harrogate, with all that, that means for the pressure on our roads, railways, housing, infrastructure, the environment, schools, hospitals and the general quality of life, it gives some idea of the scale of what Labour has bequeathed to us all."

In 2009, Andrew Neather, a former adviser to Tony Blair, Jack Straw and David Blunkett, claimed that the sharp increase in migrants over the last 10 years was partly due to a politically motivated attempt by ministers to radically change the country and "rub the 'Right's' nose in such diversity".

As already stated, what Labour has done to the nation is tantamount to treason; Oran's Dictionary of the Law (1983) defines treason as: "[a]...citizen's actions to help a foreign government overthrow, make war against, or seriously injure the [parent nation]."

In this instance, their crime has helped numerous foreign governments 'overthrow' and 'seriously injure' the country and without a bullet being fired or a foreign troop on the ground.

And to continue this 'nose rubbing' in a 'London Loves Business' article by Asa Bennett; 14 May 2013, according to Lord Mandleson, the Labour government unbelievably sent out "search parties" to get immigrants to come to work in the UK.

In May 2013, speaking at a 'Progress' conference, the former top Labour minister said: "In 2004 when as a Labour government, we were not only welcoming people to come into this country to work, we were sending out search parties for people and encouraging them, in some cases, to take up work in this country. The problem has grown during the period of economic stagnation over the last five, six years."

Due to the surge of new arrivals, Lord Mandelson said that the UK nearly became a "full employment economy", but admitted: "The situation is different obviously now." - "We have to just realise, entry to the labour market of many people of non-British origin is hard for people who are finding it very difficult to find jobs, who find it hard to keep jobs."

"For these people immigration tends to loom large in their lives and in their worlds, now that is an inescapable fact, and we have to understand it, address it, and engage with people in discussion about it," he said.

Mandleson admits there is a total-disconnect with "these people" whom he and his party are meant to be representing.

Not only do you have to question; what's really behind this type of deception? You also have to contemplate, that this is the Labour party supposedly representing the working classes; if they can cold-heartedly carry out such a brutal Brutus attack on their own indigenous working-class, then it doesn't bode well what the other parties are prepared to do and are capable of doing.

In response to these revelations, Sir Andrew Green said; "This is an astonishing admission from the highest level that Labour's mass immigration policy was entirely deliberate. It will be a very long time before their own working class supporters thank them for the enormous changes that have been imposed on their communities."

More's the pity that each and every member of the working class aren't aware of this intentional deception, and why it's equally vital that they do.

Then to really rub the noses of the so called right in diversity, when really it's just the working classes who get hurt, and then rub salt into the wounds of the injured low paid worker and unemployed; it was reported in the Telegraph on the 27 July 2013, that 814,359 jobs in the UK were being advertised to foreign workers across Europe on a website funded by the European Commission.

The website EURES had more than 1,400,000 vacancies across the EU, with the UK making up more than 50% of them.

Foreign jobseekers were also being offered up to £900 to cover travelling costs to the UK for interviews, while UK employers can receive a £1,000 bonus for taking on a non-British worker.

Yet someone unemployed in the UK would be lucky if they could get the bus fare paid to a local job interview.

UKIP's leader, Nigel Farage, said he was "astonished." - "British vacancies were being advertised abroad at a time when unemployment in the UK is rife." - "The fact that unemployed Brits are being pitted against 500 million people across the EU to get jobs in their own country is utterly reprehensible," he said.

NANNYGATE

The term 'Nannygate' came about following revelations that despite politicians professing they are deeply concerned with the matter of 'illegal immigrants' and excessive immigration in general; when it came to light in March 2014, how much MPs are fully aware of this problem - by themselves personally employing many illegal or legal migrant workers – so obviously don't even care of the impact it is having on the country.

Gita Lima, a Nepalese nanny, liked it here so much she decided to apply for British citizenship in 2010, and that her application was soon successful. Her bosses who signed her papers - are the Prime Minister David Cameron and his wife.

Number 10 denied that Samantha Cameron's support had helped speed her employee's application through the system. All procedures had been followed correctly, said a spokesman.

Yet someone as wealthy as ex Harrods boss, Al Fayed who applied for British citizenship twice - once in 1994 and once in 1999, has been refused.

Theresa May, the Home Secretary, confirmed that her cleaner was born in Brazil, and it emerged that Nick Clegg employs a Belgian.

Danny Alexander, the Chief Secretary to the Treasury, grew flustered when pressed on the radio about his family's own domestic help who too are immigrants, that no doubt many will follow the same path as Gita - and equally be successful.

A minister said: "The Cabinet is full of people who employ immigrants. For us to draw attention to this while trying to highlight concerns about immigration is not very smart."

Immigration Minister Mark Harper had to quit, when it emerged that his cleaner was an illegal immigrant.

Labour's Baroness Scotland, when Attorney General, declined to resign after being fined £5,000 for employing and illegal immigrant as a housekeeper, who was a Tongan national with no right to be in the UK.

This is why on one hand many of the middleclass view immigration as overwhelmingly positive for the economy, whilst on the other hand there are those worried about the impact on employment, public services, housing and social cohesion.

Iain Martin writes; 'So far apart are these two sides, that the protagonists might as well be talking different languages. "Metropolitan" liberals cannot see why there should be a fuss about everyone having an eastern European cleaner or getting a loft conversion carried out by Poles, while non-metropolitans marvel at the wholly false notion that everyone in Britain can afford a cleaner and a loft conversion.'

Immigration minister, Mr Brokenshire, speaking at the think-tank Demos, said: "For too long, the benefits of immigration went to employers who wanted an easy supply of cheap labour, or to the wealthy metropolitan elite who wanted cheap tradesmen and services, but not to the ordinary, hardworking people of this country."

This statement provoked fierce criticism from businesses who love slave-labour, with the head of the Institute of Directors being so annoyed by what he saw as an anti-enterprise tone of the minister's remarks, that he described the speech as "feeble and pathetic."

"There's disconnect between how immigration is viewed by affluent Londoners and by those living in less prosperous parts of Britain," said Adam Holloway, the Tory MP for Gravesham, Kent, since 2005. "The truth is that Cameron, Clegg and Miliband don't know what is happening in this country.   My constituency has been transformed since I first came to Gravesham. I don't know where these people have come from," he said.

He added that he does not blame the immigrants who are "here to get on", but he said that successive governments have "completely let down generations of working-class people" by presiding over a flawed education and training system. "If you're an employer; - who are you going to take on? These well-educated foreign workers or a less well-educated British worker?"

Mr Holloway said Britain needs to make a decision soon on whether or not it wants to control its borders: "Either we're a nation, or we're not."

The comment of not blaming immigrants who are "here to get on", is completely justifiable and understood. It's not really their fault to want to better their own lives.

If anything it could be said that the "newer arrivals" are acting like canary birds giving us an advanced warning that all is not right in Europe or the rest of the world - and that perhaps now is the time to leave the EU - otherwise we too are likely to suffocate in this process.

It's also why so called right-wing political parties such as UKIP are making such significant gains in the polls.

That if they are not destine to win the May 2015

General Election, they have a good chance of becoming a close second.

This would result in having to form a coalition government and probably with the Conservatives, for the general public now understand if they don't stand up and vote for parties like UKIP, then the situation in the UK is only going to get much worse.

It is hardly a surprise that in the run-up to the 2015 General Election, you hear inflation is at its lowest and the ONS figures allegedly show that unemployment levels have fallen in the UK to 1,860,00 million, almost 500,000 down on a year ago.

While employment allegedly increased by 103,000 to almost 3,100,000 million, said by the government to be the highest since records began in 1971.

Stating the UK now has the third lowest unemployment rate in the European Union at 5.7%.

'Unemployment – down by half a million in 2014!'

Where did all those 500,000 jobs come from - within one year?

When it's more than likely they haven't, as you'll find hundreds of thousands that were once deemed "unemployed" have been forced into going "self-employed" and receiving Universal Credits instead.

Many of these people are the one's making it appear as if 500,000 new jobs were "suddenly created."

These people receive around £15pw to £20pw less than if claiming unemployment benefit and agree to do so to escape the constant badgering from the staff at the Job Centre's who have been pressurised by the government to adopt an insensible approach towards the unemployed.

Of course there's a minority of people who know nothing else but a benefits culture, but penalising and blaming the majority for not being able to find work, despite the jobs not being there in the first place, is totally unjust.

They also feel less shamed not having to turn-up at the Job Centre and the 'Back to Work' agencies and where they have to go through the routine of being grilled all over again as to why they haven't found a job in a marketplace where over 1,007 people are applying for just eight basic non-skilled jobs at Costa Coffee or many more thousands for just forty positions at Aldi.

This means there is a sector of society who are now worse-off "pretending" to be "self-employed" when really they have no work, so just sit at home receiving less benefits than they are entitled to.

That as we now know - under Labour, the indigenous worker had 75% less chance of finding a job than their immigrant counterpart.

It's a total misconception that UK workers don't want to do "shit-jobs" (as described further on by Alex, a Romanian immigrant talking on the Channel 4 series, called the; "The Romanians Are Coming"), and only "immigrants" will do them, for as said; three quarters of those who would have applied for these such jobs, never had a chance in hell of getting them in the first place.

That's why if you look at most governmental jobs; such as social services, housing departments, Job Centre's, hospitals and council workers in general, especially 'front of house', there is a high number of immigrant workers and all thanks to Labour's 'open door' legacy to purposely try and secure 'the immigrant vote.'

They knew they'd more than likely lose the next General Election, and like they did in 2010, especially if the working-classes knew how treacherous they really had been towards those born and bred here, and no matter what their creed or colour is.

And it's far too late to resolve the problem as the devastation has already been done and why the matter is getting worse by the day.

Unless they are "illegal" immigrants you can hardly sack these workers who have been appointed these jobs.

They are not to blame, but the corrupt Labour government of the day most certainly is.

So yet again - like "they" didn't want your ancestors to know the truth about what joining the EU really meant; they certainly don't want you to know the truth about what's really going on and real state of the country, Europe and their economies - and why there are lies, damned lies and statistics!

It's as if it doesn't matter who's in government, they will always try to 'cook-the-books' so as the figures appear more palatable than they really are.

In April 2014, a number of articles appeared in the media exposing the massive increase in food banks. More than 900,000 people were given emergency food in 2013-14, an increase of 163 per cent, according to figures from the Trussell Trust, the UK's biggest food bank charity.

The explosion in demand has coincided with an increase in those seeking help following the governments benefit sanctions.

In total, 913,138 people received three days' emergency food from Trussell Trust food banks in 2013-14, compared with 346,992 in 2012-13.

And in another case of deliberate deception and lies, damned lies and statistics, in response to these appalling figures, in April 2014 the government replied;

"According the Department for Work and Pensions (DWP), a recent report by the Organisation for Economic Cooperation and Development (OECD) actually found that food poverty has gone down under this government."

Yet there's a slight oversight of the facts here - as the "recent OECD report" the DWP quoted from by the government - was actually conducted in 2012/13.

It covers April 2012 to April 2013 figures and prior to the coalition's reforms to the welfare system in which the Bedroom Tax was only first introduced in April 2013, as was the Benefit Cap.

Universal Credit was introduced in April 2014 and is still only now in 2015 being fully rolled out and applied to all of those on unemployment benefits and low incomes.

In other words, and as the independent Institute for Fiscal Studies (IFS) figures confirm, many of the government's welfare reforms had only just started when they deceptively quoted the OECD report.

What's equally shocking about these astronomically high figures, is that they are quoting only 'one' food bank charity. There are in fact over 4.7 million people living in food poverty in the UK and that the government have the bare-face-cheek in quoting 'outdated' statistics.

This is why it's almost impossible to believe whatever statistics appear in the media and especially if the source or agency are directly from or linked to the government of the day.

"LEGAL" & "UNAUTHORISED"

Despite not being able to trust many quoted government figures, they are all we can currently work from; as according to the Office for National Statistics (ONS) figures in August 2013, they reveal that the UK's population has grown by more than 400,000 to 63.7 million.

Troublingly though, these figures do not include the hundreds of thousands, if not millions of people who have smuggled themselves into the country and since 1975.

The truth is, it has been impossible to measure how many "unauthorised" people reside in the UK and will explain why in a moment.

Equally troubling, considering the significant rise of immigrants entering the country in just the past three years, is that the total number of migrants that arrived in the UK in the year 2014 alone, was 624,000, - the highest on record.

The ONS announced a net flow of 298,000 migrants to the UK in the 12 months to last September 2014, – up from 210,000 in the previous year, and equal to the population of a city like Nottingham and a total of 508,000 in just two years.

Producing enough citizen for another city almost the same size and quicker than they could build a housing estate to house just 100,000.

This means David Cameron failed abysmally in his pledge to reduce the net flow of immigrants.

To try and help ease these disturbing figures, it's said 327,000 emigrated. Yet this figure has to be disputed, which in turn could place the 298,000 figure even higher. Perhaps they are correct, but with all the previous and present governments deceptive quoting of such figures and as already proven so far; it's difficult to believe them, and here's perhaps why;

On BBC Question Time the 26 February 2015, according to one of the guest panelists, Liberal Democrat Tessa Munt MP, she said along the lines; "...we ought to start registering the true number of "emigrants", those leaving the country, as presently there is no such system and we have no real idea of how many are leaving."

According to Lord Green of Deddington, chairman of Migration Watch UK; "Incredible though it may seem, these (no exist checks) have not been in operation for 20 years. As a result, the Government has no idea whatsoever who is on this island. Exit controls, due at last to come into effect next May 2016, will make a start on that."

"For example, non-EU students are a major concern. Despite a barrage of propaganda from the education sector, the fact is that they have been arriving at the rate of about 150,000 a year, but only 50,000 a year are leaving," he said.

So where did the ONS get this 327,000 figure from? Who can we really trust?

I think it could be fair to assume that the British general public have long be lied to about how many immigrants truly are residing in the UK.

No doubt sometime in the future, perhaps after and if the present government lose the forthcoming General Election, the British public may find out that these figures had also been fabricated so as to not make the actual net figures appear more worse than they actually are.

What's also troubling, is that the following data is between five and ten years old; Labour was in power and it was obviously not in their interest to conduct such research.

Not surprising, though it has proven to be difficult to source more recent and accurate statistics - that think-tanks such as Migration Watch UK have long disputed, saying; '...they are underestimated,' and we tend to agree.

A Home Office study based on 2001 Census data released in March 2005, estimated an unauthorised population of between 310,000 and 570,000.

In 2011, a study carried out by a research team at London School of Economics (LSE) for the Greater London Authority, estimated undocumented migrants oscillate between 417,000 and 863,000, including a population of UK-born children ranging between 44,000 and 144,000.

Drawing-on this and taking stock of the outcome of a Case Resolution Programme, a University of Oxford's study by Nando Sigona and Vanessa Hughes, estimate at the end of 2011 a population of undocumented migrant children of 120,000, with over half born in the UK to parents residing without legal immigration status.

As cited, Migration Watch UK have criticised the Home Office figures, suggesting they have underestimated the numbers of unauthorised migrants by between 15,000 and 85,000.

Jack Dromey, Deputy General of the Transport and General Workers Union and Labour Party treasurer, suggested in May 2006, that there could be around 500,000 "illegal" workers. He called for a public debate on whether an amnesty should be considered.

When Home Secretary, David Blunkett - suggested that this might be done once the "identity card scheme" was rolled out in 2006.

However, despite its introduction in 2006, the Identity Documents Act 2010 (c. 40) Act of Parliament introduced by the coalition government reversed the introduction of identity cards and required the destruction of the information held on the National Identity Register.

As a Bill, it was presented to the House of Commons by Home Secretary Theresa May on 26 May 2010.

Though what cannot be overlooked, is the matter that why wasn't Jack Dromey, David Blunkett, et al - more concerned about the 500,000 "illegal immigrants" who are here working and depriving half a million indigenous workers from doing so?

London Citizens, a coalition of community organisations, runs a regularisation campaign called; 'Strangers into Citizens', backed by figures including the leader of the Catholic Church in England and Wales, the Cardinal Cormac Murphy-O'Connor.

Analysis by the Institute for Public Policy Research suggested that an amnesty would net the government up to £1.038 billion per year in fiscal revenue.

The Mayor of London, Boris Johnson commissioned a study into a possible amnesty for illegal immigrants, citing larger tax gains within the London area which is considered to be home to the majority of the country's population of such immigrants.

However, once again they conveniently seem to overlook one important factor, apart from denying those born here such work opportunities; analysis by Migration Watch UK suggests that if the migrants were granted amnesty, given access to healthcare and other benefits, the net cost to the exchequer would be £5.530 billion annually.

"They" seem to love bantering about all the plus-points, yet don't like to look deeper into the reality of it all and the disastrous affects it's having on the indigenous working classes already living here.

On the 25 July 2013, the National Census Statistics were released, and prior to Romania and Bulgaria joining the EU in 2014, and the recent net migration figures of 298,000 were announced.

Previous data shows that in the year ending September 2014 an estimated 37,000 citizens from Romania and Bulgaria migrated to the UK, while 4,000 left, though again these figures have to be taken with a pinch of salt as we believe the incoming number to be higher, and as said we have no idea whose leaving the UK.

And regardless that the number of families on the waiting list for social housing stood at a record 1.8million; of the 4,000,000 immigrants who arrived in the UK between 2001 and 2011, it said 469,843 of them were given council or housing association properties.

Around 1.2million immigrants now live in social housing – one in eight of the total. In London the figure is thought to be as high as one in five.

Then there's just as many, if not more living in private accommodation and where the rents and council tax is being paid by the benefits system and why landlords are charging such high "guaranteed" rents.

This is why "Buy to Let" schemes have made a

handful of landlord's millionaires in comparison to non-home-owners, whilst driving the property prices up and creating a shortage of them in the same process.

According to the 'Ilford Recorder' - on 19 February 2015, it reported that Cllr Jas Athwal, leader of the Labour-run Redbridge Council; had accused Westminster City Council of "dumping" their poorest residents in the borough - after it emerged they were buying properties in Redbridge to house its homeless - that in most cases are Romanian descent and were round-up by the police in places like Park Lane. Westminster City revealed it purchased 10 properties in Redbridge over the past 18 months to use as temporary accommodation, each costing an average of £183,000.

Like so many London boroughs, Redbridge reported some of the 8,000 families on their housing waiting list were having to be housed in faraway places - such as Birmingham and Slough.

"Westminster see east London as a cheap option because you can buy a house for £200,000, where the same house could be £2 million there. Most of the boroughs are doing it, because the system is so fragmented and so broken," said Jas Athwal.

Yet what Jas the Labour councilor forgot to mention, was where did these additional poorest residents from Westminster originate from?

And then there's the question of his own party's open-door policy and why we have another case of the kettle calling the pot black.

The European Commission (EC) have expanded their bottomless pit of colossal budgets, pushing Britain's disproportionate contributions even higher and with Brussels continuous job-destroying proposals, (e.g. advertising those 800,000+ jobs in the UK on their own website in Europe) over regulation, their own unemployment issues, austerity measures and turning the whole of the EU into a zone of high taxation; that it's no wonder the desperate populations of these members states are doing all they can to flee their countries of origin and seek sanctuary elsewhere – and in most cases, the UK.

To fully appreciate the fact that "they" never wanted our predecessors to fully understand what it really meant by Great Britain joining the Common Market; – the Treaty of Rome was actually forced upon the general public without the referendum they were originally promised by the then three main political parties.

Time and again they were hoodwinked and lied to.

Apart from UKIP, none of the major parties have a credible plan to reduce immigration and whilst the UK remain in the EU, they cannot do anything about it - and why they should stop play-acting that they can.

With the EU playing an ever more dominant role in border control issues, leaving its member states powerless to control migrant flows, not only from other EU countries, but from much further abroad such as the Canada, USA, S. America, Africa, Asia, China and Russia too, then matters will escalate and get even worse.

The Free Movement of Labour clause within the Treaty of Rome was like much else, played down. Many members of the public were totally unware of its true implications - that makes this influx of mass immigration impossible to prevent.

The fact of the matter is that ever since the ratification of the Treaty of Rome: Free Movement of Labour - Articles (48 to 73), that has remained in all the subsequent treaties; under European Law no one requires a passport to travel within the member states of the EU.

This is why it's been pure theatre as to why people have been led to believe they require a passport, and probably done so as to avoid an earlier outrage; if say they are wanting to work (thus live) in any European member state, as "legally" they don't and never have needed to require one; - as after all that's the whole meaning and objective of Articles 48 to 73 of the Free Movement of Labour clause.

On the europa.eu website, under "Travel documents for EU nationals" it states: If you are an EU national, you do not need to show your national ID card or passport when you are travelling from one border-free Schengen EU country to another.

That within itself creates an anomaly, for as soon as someone arrives at a "Schengen" border, if ever asked, they can simply lie and just say they come from another European country. And because no documentation is required, the authorities would be none the wiser.

The 26 Schengen areas are all the main countries and member states of the European Union, other than Bulgaria, Croatia, Cyprus, Ireland, Romania and the United Kingdom - in which: "You must still show a valid ID card or passport."

You will note the word "or", meaning a national ID card will suffice, including a European driving licence.

It's just a matter of time before these other member states also become part of the Schengen area.

Basically and as stated 'any person from a member state of the EU' just simply requires a valid (easy to fake) ID card and if they turned up at a UK border with just that and without a passport, then entry cannot be refused otherwise the UK Border Agency will be in-breech of Articles 48 to 73.

The Schengen Agreement led to the creation of Europe's borderless Schengen Area in 1995.

The treaty was signed on 14 June 1985 between five of the then ten member states of the European Economic Community near the town of Schengen in Luxembourg.

This is hardly a new amendment; as all that really happened when coming to the Schengen Agreement, was that they were recognising and upholding Articles 48 to 73 of the Free Movement of Labour clause and implementing it as so.

It proposed the gradual abolition of border checks at the signatories' common borders.

Measures proposed include reduced speed vehicle checks which allows vehicles to cross borders without stopping, allowing of residents in border areas freedom to cross borders away from fixed checkpoints and the harmonisation of visa policies.

So we reiterate; this is why so many people can enter the UK with the simplest of identification, such as a European driving licence or ID card, both deemed as "valid" ID cards.

That in turn has made it easier for those living outside the EU to also gain entry by using the most simplest of fraudulent documentation.

As mentioned earlier; it was reported in the media 1 February 2014, that Ministers actual conspired and 'hid' evidence of migrants abusing EU rules and defrauding the British benefits system with fake documentation and saying they were related to European families and as MPs were debating the

Immigration Bill.

In the most extreme cases, criminal gangs have trafficked people into Britain and forced them to beg on the streets and open bank accounts in order to claim welfare, before withdrawing the money and leaving them destitute.

And that due to it appearing that many members of the British public still don't really understand what the articles in the 'treaties' mean or what the European Union really represents and the disadvantages it has on their livelihoods as a whole; is why it was decided to write this book and also include an updated evaluation of; *Joining the Common Market or What the Treaty of Rome Means.*

This 14 page small booklet was first published in 1967 to try and inform your ancestors, alive or since deceased, with tit-bits of information from the Treaty of Rome and in layman terms as to what kind of predicament the country was being sleepwalked into.

(You will read within its opening the following; "...probably very few hon. Members, and certainly the vast majority of people in the country have never read this document. I am afraid that many Ministers and ex-Ministers have never read it." - Sir Harry Legge-Bourke, MP - 16th November, 1966.)

That in many respects has come true and that without doubt has totally altered the dynamics of the country and to such an extent that it is barely recognisable in some quarters and sectors of society.

In 1967 and like that of today, the majority of members from the main three political parties were all singing from the same song sheet and serenading the gullible British public into an arrangement that they had hardly any understanding of its melody.

For far too long, it is the 1% and their army of politicians and lobbyist who are behind the types of pro-conglomerate-multinational-political groups and organisations – in whose interest it is - is to make sure that profits remain high as can be, wages kept as low as possible and for tax revenues to be forever imposed on the man-in-the-street, as opposed to the multimillion pound making conglomerates and banking institutions.

That alongside thousands more hangers-on riding the same gravy-train of quango set-ups and NGO type of groups and organisations that keep a select group of see no evil, hear no evil - or speak nothing of all the corruption that's going on around them in a their secure, all expenses paid for golden-handshake cushy number jobs; is how such a gigantic white-elephant like the European Commission is kept alive and in existence for so long - despite all its obvious failings.

And that whenever there is any sign of discontent or "they" come under fire from those protesting that their standards of living is lower than it was forty years ago, and that without doubt the main cause of this is simply because there are far too many people in the country and that the infrastructure is no longer in place; "they" have the audacity to produce the 'race card', often branding their critics as racists.

Hoping it will then silence them and that they will soon go away.

This tactic has worked time and again. Yet as a nation you have to confront this momentous concern with an hands-on approach. As a collective, you all have to recognise this major problem isn't going to go away and if ignored for much longer, it will of course get so much worse.

This is why it needs addressing and tackling now this coming general election and before it really is too late.

Of course you can let another 5 or 10 million or more enter the country, but can you imagine what the conditions and standard of living will be like?

It's almost as if the 1% are determine to impose a type of Dickensian lifestyle onto masses.

You have to learn to understand that you are not enemies like you've probably been led to believe, as the vast majority – the working classes – are all in the same boat.

This is not a matter of finger pointing and has to be dealt with in the most dignified of ways.

Combined, you have to comprehend you have all

become victims of a social experiment - gone wrong.

And that the only ones to really benefit and who already have done so from the development of the European Union are the 1%, and perhaps a sector of the middle-classes – who are in many of the self-appointed ("or elected") cushy-number-jobs as mentioned elsewhere.

It's further argued, that instead and since the British public were railroaded into joining the EU in 1973, along with a handful of bureaucrat's riding the European gravy train-surmounting to one power grub after another, introducing over-regulation, all-round interference and now at a time of austerity throughout Europe, - that this is the real reason there is so much upheaval and uncertainty on the continent and why again a European army is being called for.

Perhaps this alone is why Great Britain should leave the European Union now and before it totally goes to wrack and ruin.

"THEY" LOVE IT WHEN YOU DON'T VOTE

As this is another ploy of the 1%, that despite it may appear "they" are concerned that not enough people are voting, this mainly applies to the middle-classes.

"They" love it when the working-classes complain and question; "They're all the same, so why bother voting?"

For "they" have devised it that way.

Don't forget your ancestors, especially women, weren't simply given the vote, it was fought for. Hundreds of thousands, if not millions (worldwide) have died in the process of gaining it.

Your world governments have long been infiltrated by cartels and by the sorts American President John F Kennedy was warning the world about - and if for any reason - this was probably why he was assassinated.

Up until now and for the past hundred years or more it's always been a two, perhaps three horse race, though the Liberals have never really been a serious contender.

"They" have always sat easy knowing that it doesn't matter who wins an election, the slave-working-class electorate would be getting somewhat the same type of government, - other than a few tweaks here and few "changes" there, though nevertheless the same political system and retroact remains and whereas nothing really changes.

It's mainly the middle-classes who vote, often wasting their vote on political parties such as the Liberals or Green Party.

Whilst others, mainly the well-off, have voted Conservative.

Of course many others vote for Labour, though they relied on the 'union vote' and working-classes.

Yet after experiencing their "open-door policy" and decades of what has happened to the miner's union, the print, the transportation union and privatisation of the railways and utility companies in general and done so with the help of corrupt bosses and union representatives, they totally lost all hope and respect for the so called party who was meant to be representing them.

And again you have to realise it was cleverly devised that way and why it can't and doesn't happen overnight, but took a succession of deliberate incompetent governments to get the country to this stage.

That's why Labour have more chance of succeeding with the immigrant vote as opposed to gaining the downtrodden indigenous working class vote they once took for granted and enjoyed.

The is why the country (Europe/world) is on the precipice of fundamental change, - if only the working classes were to wake-up and realise - that at no time before has their vote held so much sway and power over the lives of the very people who have ruined, not only their lives, but their descendants and their own children's lives as well. Though it's still not too late for them to help change the outcome.

Democracy, alongside good transparent honest government and a capitalistic/socialist joint system in place that's not all about profit for the few but profit for all, can be achieved.

Perhaps there are better political systems and ideas yet to come, though you can't expect to suddenly change eons of genuine democracy; a tribalism primitive democracy as identified in small communities or villages when the following takes place; face-to-face discussions in the village council or a headman/women whose decisions are then supported by the people showing of hands-voting and their village elders or other cooperative modes of government paying heed and implementing such decisions and for the betterment of everyone - and not just for a small percentage of society.

For when this does not happen it often means genuine democracy has failed and a sharper, darker contrast arises and other forms of rule come into play, monarchy, tyranny, aristocracy, and oligarchy - and what sadly is currently flourishing the world over today - and has done for thousands of years.

That's why "they" don't want to give it back so easily.

Yet the real power is in the hands of the people, it always has been and will be - solely due to their sheer numbers – that if they really acted as a collective – the 1% would have nowhere to go.

And until this moment in time, "they" and "you" were and are right, "their" and "your" vote was useless and meant nothing in regards to change; - yet by voting for a party that promises to leave the

EU, thus ripping-up the failed "Treaty of Rome" and its subsequent treaties, along with the Free Movement of Labour clauses, "they" and "you" might be able to alter the course of history - and for the benefit of all mankind - and not just a few.

And that after witnessing such a valiant and courageous move being enacted by the British electorate other European countries could soon to follow suit.

Recognising their own countries have also been taken over by the same corrupt cartels whose only real interest is to empower the 1% even more and until "they" own almost all the planet and its resources - and to the total detriment of its people.

It's up to you and your "brothers" and "sisters" around the world to do the same in your and their own countries, as this is the only true answer, - home is where the heart is and there's a reason for that.

Don't let "them" chase you out of "your" town, steal your land, resources and destroy your hearts in the same process, fight-back and vote!

Rid your nations of these greedy, corrupt cartels for if you don't do it now, then you, your children and your children's children will never even experience true "freedom" - something we should all be entitled to and no matter where we live or come from.

Though it can only ever really be achieved by first gaining it from the place you first came from.

Running away doesn't solve the problem; like you have to learn to love yourself before you can others, the same applies to your origins – and until this is achieved, "man" will always have that empty inner-feeling – that you 'still haven't found what you are looking for...'

Travelling the world is great when done for all the right reasons. But if your country is in turmoil, then it probably needs you. It's only "the people" who can really change things and that can only be achieved as a collective and at home.

In the 21st century there is no reason whatsoever as to why all countries don't have better social housing, schools, hospital, business and the infrastructure in place and the only reason they haven't is not because lack of funds or resources, but because corruption by their 1%.

And it is these people who are the enemy to man and no matter where he comes from.

We all have to understand, that to gain real freedom from a group hell bent in not wanting to grant it to us, then it's never going to be an easy ride to obtain this freedom and equality and no matter where you are in the world.

TV organisations such as the BBC, have long been known for their social engineering range of soaps and TV drama's conditioning the masses as to how things "should be" within society and within "their" eyes – that often seems pro-paedophilia and why some much of it exists in the UK.

They are of course equally famous for their propagandist 'points of view'.

Knowing that the question of immigration and whether the country should leave the EU is high-up on the list of conversations taking place up and down the country, and more so in the run-up to the 2015 General Election;

the BBC, like that of Channel 4 and Channel 5 seem to have decided to politicise their "entertainment schedules" by investing more time and money than they normally would by making a whole series of programmes related to the issues of immigration.

It makes you question as to what their own hidden agenda really is. For as you'll notice all of their films and shows are pro-EU and immigration.

Not one of them has tried to come from an angle of the "complainant", who you'll find are the majority viewer of their programmes.

They are therefore abusing their positions as broadcasters, especially the licence fee charging

BBC, by blatantly promoting propaganda as opposed to trying to achieve an equilibrium and showing both sides of the argument.

First 100 Days of UKIP; - a "mockudrama" aired on the 16 February 2015, about the rising of Nigel Farage to number 10 after his party wins the General Election.

Probably using a mixture of genuine film footage from the UK riots that took place around the country after the 2011 shooting of Mark Duggan, in Tottenham, London, or following the student protests in 2010 over the stoppage of tuition fees, also in London - and of course actors; the "play" depicts riots taking place and groups of protesters for and against tough anti-immigration laws.

It also features a factory closing-down as a direct result of the UK withdrawing from the EU.

The programme featured actress Priyanga Burford playing the part of the party's only Asian woman MP. Her character Deepa, is elected to serve for Romford in an imagined landslide victory by UKIP, that then seems to portray her grappling with her conscience amid a hypothetically UKBA (UK-Border Agency) raid and the factory closure based in her own constituency.

As part of a PR exercise, you see Deepa going on a UKBA raid at an address were its claimed there's a hive of illegal immigrants hiding out.

The raid goes wrong and in the process a young man is injured by the UKBA officers. To make matters worse he is then falsely accused of 'assault' on one of the arresting officers.

Deepa witnessed the assault, but chose to remain silent about it.

Viewers who watched the film would have seen that Deepa didn't change her stance in regards to being an MP for UKIP. The grappling with her conscience was witnessing "UKBA-police brutality" in which she was keeping quiet about.

This has been going on for decades and under the watch of most previous governments. The witnessing of any type of "police brutality" and being pressurised to help cover it up would have got to most people's conscience.

The problem was not so much UKIP or their policies, in which the film tried to portray, if anything it seems to endorse the police and no matter who the government of the day may be, are as brutal as they are allowed to be and perhaps it's the laws and their procedures that need to be relooked into and changed.

In regards to the factory closure, some will recall what both Labour and Tories did to the UK's manufacturing and producing sectors; the coal miners, car-makers, print and the privatisation of the utilities and train companies that led to 100,000s of redundancies.

Ironically, it was mainly the founding of the EU, that destroyed Fords of Dagenham, that borders the borough of Romford and why the former town even exists as most people worked there and from both those areas and why "Fords" built it so as their workers were on the doorstep.

In 1960s, Ford finally began to merge its previously competing British and German subsidiaries, culminating in the creation of Ford of Europe in 1967.

Following a series of industrial actions because production of the Ford Escort was lost by Dagenham and made at the new Saarlouis factory in West Germany, the Dagenham plant was finally closed down resulting to thousands being made redundant and unemployed.

Through Labour's own admission, they clearly gave preference to migrants workers as opposed to those born in the UK.

So without doubt, it was an over exaggeration of how it could be if UKIP won the 2015 General Election.

UKIP MEP and parliamentary candidate Gerald Batten, told LBC Radio: "I'm not quite sure what you would describe it as, apart from a piece of bile and vitriol from our political opponents, who don't happen to be in a political party – they're in a TV channel and don't have to go through the inconvenience of running for office. They can just spout their views and don't actually have to go out and defend them in elections, which we do."

The UKBA introduced a civil penalty system for employers on 29 February 2008, as part of the Asylum and Nationality Act 2006. £10,000 fines for employers found to be employing illegal immigrants where there is negligence on the part of the employer, with unlimited fines or jail sentences for employers acting knowingly.

Yet this hasn't helped stem the flow or tackle the problem as there are so many ways to get around it. Often the "boss" is 'out of the country' and never gets prosecuted.

Though a more common practice, is that false documentation is used, therefore the onus is no longer on the employer, despite them knowing the paperwork must be false, they technically cannot be prosecuted.

In July 2013, and as mentioned elsewhere, the Home Office introduced an advertising lorry driving around the streets of London with a billboard reading; "In the UK illegally? — GO HOME OR FACE ARREST — Text HOME to 78070 for free advice and help with travel documents. We can help you return home voluntarily without fear of arrest or detention."

This campaign was criticised from various quarters: Vince Cable, a prominent Liberal Party minister in the governing coalition, called it "stupid and offensive" some on the left said that "Go Home" evoked an old National Front slogan.

And much to the surprise of the media, Nigel Farage also criticised the campaign as "nasty" and suggested that its real message was; "Please don't vote UKIP, we're doing something".

You could therefore assume that if Mr Farage found that offensive and "nasty", that he would make sure his own party went about tackling the issue of mass immigration as humanly and sophisticated as possible. For if they don't the British electorate will not tolerate it and they will be out of office as fast as they were voted in.

Interestingly, it was around the same period of time, the mid 1960s, when the debate over whether the UK should join the Common Market, that the BBC first aired Johnny Speight's, Till Death Us Do Part; a television sitcom that ran from 1965 to 1975; it started two years prior to the 'Joining the Common Market or What the Treaty of Rome Means' booklet was first printed in 1967 - and ended the same year a 'Yes'- 'No' referendum was held in the UK on whether the country should remain in the EU.

So it was primed and timed just right to work on the psyche of the "British" public.

Till Death Us Do Part centred on the East End of London Garnett family, led by patriarch Alf Garnett (Warren Mitchell), a reactionary white working-class man who held racist and anti-socialist views.

It could be contended that it was specifically commissioned by the BBC to help tackle the concerns over joining the Common Market, for like that of today, back then in the 1960s there was those who too could see the disadvantages in joining a European Union and were strongly opposed to it.

And again, back then it was generally the media who often accused these dissenting voices as being racists and not looked upon as genuinely concerned individuals worried that there simply will not be enough jobs, homes or the infrastructure in place to cope with all the additional millions of immigrants who will "legally" be permitted to enter the UK, and who have since arrived and proved their concerns to be totally justified.

The Romanians Are Coming, was a documentary aired on Channel 4, 24 February 2015. It ostensibly tried to explore the reality of life in Romania and the motivation driving Romanians to the UK.

It showed a middle-class female nurse named Mihalia, and a 30 year old working-class man called Alex, who was sleeping rough inside a cardboard box in some bushes in Sheppard's Bush, London.

The gypsy Romanian narrator, also named Alex, sarcastically states; '…how come guys like Alex, living on the streets can get a job in a factory, easier than someone from the UK?'

It was obviously orchestrated by the programme makers who clearly had a hidden agenda, which was trying to portray the British as being lazy and not wanting to do such jobs, thus justifying Alex being here.

Yet they overlooked one vital matter, which is the 'wages' and how low they are to survive on and why Alex and others like him were having to live on the streets, as they too can't afford to pay the rents in London if working for such low pay.

The same applies to those working and living in rented accommodation with many migrant workers having to share a home with up to ten or more other migrant workers, so they can afford to pay the rents and bills.

26 February 2015, on the Labour Party's website they reported the number of homeless people sleeping on the streets has risen by almost a thousand since David Cameron became Prime Minister. Latest figures show that there were 2,744 people rough sleeping in autumn 2014, compared to 1,768 in 2010.

Shadow Housing Minister Emma Reynolds said the rise recorded in these figures was "shocking" and condemned the policies that has led to the worsening situation.

"Rising housing costs and low pay have made it more and more difficult for people to keep a roof over their head. The Tory-led Government has presided over the lowest levels of house building in peacetime since the 1920s, a drop in the number of affordable homes being built and policies like the Bedroom Tax have made things even worse."

It was only a matter of weeks when Alex was then sacked from his warehouse job for turning up drunk for work. It also turned out he had done the same in the USA, so hardly the best of workers or as destitute as the programme was trying to portray he was.

It's a shame more British men or women didn't have the same opportunity as Alex, which was to travel through Europe and the world in hope of finding work.

Mihalia, blamed her pay was being delayed and she was being paid lower than other workers because she was Romanian.

Though this sounds more like an excuse and was probably due to her not completing the six months she agreed to do with the nursing agency and returned home earlier to her family, including her 80 year old mother who she was worried about if something was to happen to her health whilst she was working away.

The programme's producers also expertly seem to cast and include the worse bunch of "white-English/British" citizens they could muster-up to appear on the screen and who looked more like someone out of the inbred cast from the Hollywood film 'Deliverance'.

One young man briefly appears tar-brushing all Romanians as being thieves; '...who steal from your back garden and start fights in the street,' - who quite comically goes on to say; "They are dirty, nasty, horrible people."

That along with his cataract in one eye, scarred face and badly shaped nicotine stained teeth, you could have easily thought he was describing himself, - and that of course was the programme maker's intention.

Immediately following The Romanians Are Coming, Channel 4 screened another documentary, titled; Immigration Street. It was meant to have been a thought provoking film giving a unique insight into the reality of multiculturalism in Britain today, capturing contemporary life on an ethnically diverse street in a southern seaport-town.

Whilst most people would have hoped that after all the controversy that surrounded their Benefits Street series, it would have deterred Channel 4 from wanting to interfere with local communities again, instead they decided to take it that one step further and all the way to Derby Road in Southampton.

They tried to portray it was the "ethnic diversity" of this seaport side-street that made it something out of the ordinary with its residents living in perfect harmony.

Yet it soon backfired on the programme makers, as it was solely due to them that such discord was created in the first place.

Nor is it that uncommon of a street that you'll find in most towns, other than its probably completely alien to the kind of place or street the middleclass film-crew perhaps come from.

In many parts of the UK, especially in other seaside towns or cities and particularly in places like London, Birmingham, Leicester or Bradford, you'll find 1000s of "Derby Road's."

You may well have seen or read about the subsequent spectacle that took place during and after the filming of Immigrant Street, as local residents and political campaigners put pressure on Channel 4 to axe the fly-on-the-wall show.

In fact local gangs of thugs set-upon the film crew, threatening to beat them-up or even shoot them.

Some "residents" who agreed to appear in the film were attacked and badly injured.

Though here's the paradox of what really took place; those "immigrants" who took offence and chased the film crew out of town, thought the producers were there to 'name and shame them'.

To put them in a bad light and paint a bad picture of them as being some kind of 'spongers off the state' and who were here to steal the indigenous peoples jobs, housing and women.

When anyone who knows how the BBC and Channel 4 really work and their hidden agendas, they would have known that simply wasn't the case and the outcome would have been pro-immigration.

That as much as the producers desperately wanted to be able to explain to the residents who took offence to their presence and filming of the street they lived on;

they could hardly confess and tell the worlds media who by now had heard of all the "racial tension" erupting on Derby Road, so too descended on the street in their droves; that the real reasons for making 'Immigration Street', was quite the opposite of what the residents first believed and that their hidden agenda was to shame the British indigenous public by yet again suggesting they were lazy good for nothing racists and not prepared to work.

Whilst on the other hand, the forever grateful "immigrants" are hard grafters and beneficial to the country.

Had they called it 'Diversity Street', then maybe the residents wouldn't have been so offended.

Rafique, a local businessman who appears in the film, claimed his family came over in the 50s and not the 70's after the Ugandan president, Idi Amin, in August 1972, declared what he called an "economic war" and expelled over 60,000 Asians (some of them held British passports) and who many ended up in the UK.

When only 15yrs old, Rafique's father died and he inherited the family business. Rafique has a large number of houses in Derby Road that he rents out to "immigrants" who emigrated from places like Somalia, Jamaica, Pakistan, India, and the Middle East - for over four decades, thus from the 70's era onwards. You'll note most of the "immigrants" are not even from Eurozone countries.

Some local residents we spoke to - claimed Rafique of being racist - as he didn't rent his properties out to "white English/British born tenants".

When asked; "Why was this the case? They replied; "It's because 'we' expect and demand too much. Such as when the boiler breaks down or the place needs redecorating, perhaps due to damp and we'd like it sorted out. Whereas the immigrants are just happy to have a roof over their heads and not complain."

Rafique, states on the film; "You want the truth? English people are very lazy, the immigrants come in, do all the hard work and rubbish jobs and they do well and you people can't handle it, and that's the honest truth. That ten to fifteen years down the line they are doing well, while those sitting on their arse's complaining; - why are these people doing well?" "And if it wasn't for the immigrants after world war two, your country, well our country, wouldn't be where it is today. You still be there with your Fish and Chip shops, closing at twelve o'clock, opening back at two, closed on Sunday's all day, - what you reckon?"

There were many pubs, clubs and shops up and down Great Britain that had no particular set routine of closing and especially pre WWII. Ronnie Barkers sitcom series - Open All Hours, was a reflection of those days.

It was due to the war that they needed men and women to fight and make ammunitions, therefore didn't want the nation drinking all night in the pub and why closing times were introduced. The same applied after the war as they needed to rebuild the country after worn torn Britain had been bomb so much, including Southampton.

Throughout time Great Britain has always been open for business, shops and all. In the 1930s there were many late evening/night cafes and 24hr restaurants, even on railway stations, and it wasn't until the introduction of Cannabis in the 1960s that the local authorities began to get worried that gangs of "mods, rockers and Teddy-boys" and then "hippies" would be hanging-out and congregating until the late hours of the evening, that a "Premises Licence" was introduced and required and café's had to close early if not granted one.

Being a predominately Christian society, Sunday was the "day of rest", many still view it as so, and it was "illegal" to trade on that day. It still is at certain times on Sunday. Yet what many non-Christian shop-keepers started to do was to simply ignore the law and disrespect the 'day of rest' as it didn't concern them.

Many small shops were family run businesses and they often lived above the shop. Closing for "lunch" gave them time to eat as well.

Non-Muslim Britain's are disadvantaged when it comes to loaning money, say for opening a small business. They have to have good credit and rely on a bank to loan them the money. Whereas the vast majority of Muslim people can go to their local Mosque and seek help that way.

This perhaps isn't normally the case to set-up large scale businesses. But like Jewish people, Muslims don't believe in Usury, so often get financial help this way – yet "normal" society accepts this injustice.

In fact it's a great idea. One the churches should have long adopted as perhaps they too would have more worshipers if they did. It's more built on trust and commitment and in a sense you're lending from the "community" as opposed to some big bank and therefore feel more connected and caring about those who lent you the funds to start your business. It's less sterile than "normal" banking practices, a lot cheaper and don't normally put a "charge" on your home.

What the wider public perhaps didn't see or even know about the film company Love Productions, makers of Benefits Street and Immigrants Street; that what other residents in the street soon got wind-off, was that they could soon see for themselves and that resulted to the inevitable clash and attacks on these other "residents" and the film crew themselves, is that it appears certain things were stage managed.

According to some of those we spoke to since the making of the film and who are residents of Derby Road, it appears "film extras" were drafted in.

People just appeared on the scene, yet were being featured in the film. Flags were all of a sudden being seen put up in various windows representing the nations they came from.

Delroy, was one of those and he could be seen sticking-up a Jamaican flag in his own window. One of the local residents who confronted the film crew and claimed, unlike Delroy, that he had lived there for over 30yrs and accused Delroy of being a plant, an outsider.

And when accusing Delroy of being so and asking him where exactly did he come from - and if he preferred they could talk in their Jamaican dialogue, known as "Patois", Delroy refused and wouldn't answer him. Other than he said - it was Rafique who arranged it. Delroy was "living" in one of Rafique's properties.

You would have thought that if Delroy was genuine and had lived there for ex-amount of time, then surely he would have defended himself and said so, but he didn't.

It's been claimed that since the filming stopped, Delroy moved away.

One other scene in the show depicts a Portuguese family, headed by Nuno, who said he had noticed the empty house and offered the landlord to freely renovate the place in exchange of being allowed to move in.

And in good stead to help drive-home Love Productions message and hidden agenda; Nuno went on to say, "I sometimes feel I'm not welcome here, just because I'm from an EU country." "It's like what they did in Nazi Germany, they blamed the Jew's. The retroact is still the same. People blame the foreigners for everything, it is racism in-it."

They then show a close-up of an UKIP advert on Nuno's Ipad phone; it's of a builder sitting down on the pavement during a tea-break. It reads: "EU policy at work" – "British workers are hit hard with unlimited cheap labour."

Nuno scoffs at it, and says; "That's not the reality, if British workers are out of work it's probably because they are not good enough. He's sitting down, not doing any work, maybe if he didn't have so many tea-breaks he wouldn't be out of work," – and laughs.

Out of the white English people who appeared in the film, they said they were scared to raise their voices in case they were called a racist. And that they were not racist and just cared about the future of the country.

For sure there are many more potential undecided "shy-voters" in the UK, who are either far too reserved or in fear of being branded a "racist" if they openly admitted they are warming to party's such as UKIP.

On the 4 March 2015, it seems Channel 5 couldn't escape the media's craze of wishing to undermine Nigel Farage and UKIP voters that a brand new documentary was aired supposedly looking at those who support UKIP; from fisherman who say that their livelihoods are being destroyed by EU legislation to those who blame immigration for the UK's ills.

The programme was titled; Farage Fans and UKIP Lovers.

It's almost as if they are trying every angle they can to expose UKIP voters as racist and fail each time. You can't blame a political party for who may vote for them, especially out of population of 63 million.

And why again it's the 1% who own the media who are trying their upmost to say; "...you must be a raving lunatic to vote UKIP," - knowing this type of programme would yet again attract sensationalised headlines such as: 'Watch the extraordinary rant by a man who wants to HARVEST paedophiles for their organs', as that's what the Mirror did.

They showed extracts of the documentary on their own website promoting the Channel 5 film being aired that same night.

There was a chap named Roget, who stated: "I've never voted before but this time I'm voting UKIP because I believe they can make a change. I firmly believe that they are going to put Britain first."

He was asked about his stance on the death penalty and replied; "If someone 'takes a children's life' then they should lose theirs. Not put in prison and looked after. Preposterous!" - "If paedophiles organs are good enough, they should be used and when ill children need them. Because they've abused the right to live and carry on in our society –

and society and the community is what makes us all tick."

Roget defends his comments; "My views here may be classed as extremist, but to me they're common sense."

Fishermen father and son team, Terry and Luke of Folkestone are anti-EU and want the UK out of Europe because of the EU's fishing quotas and killing off British fishing. They think UKIP can save the day.

There's also London cabbie Graham Long, whose says; "Some politicians are afraid to be English. They're frightened to say what a lot of people want to say."

They then show Claire Khaw, a self-confessed internet troll and a former member of the BNP. Despite her supporting UKIP, the party refuse to let her join because of her BNP connection.

This perhaps says a lot more about UKIP than it does by including someone like her in this anti-UKIP programme.

Can you imagine Channel 5 interviewing the thousands, if not hundreds of thousands of members of the public who are voters of the three main political parties and what a mishmash bunch of people they'd find!

Not to mention all the scandalous paedophile accusations said to involve members of parliament, Liberal MP Cyril Smith comes to mind, along with many other politicians and local councilors up and down the country who have been found guilty of the most horrendous of crimes;

according to Andrew Gilligan of the Telegraph on the 15 March 2015: "Dolphin Square is not the only way the story of a claimed Westminster "abuse conspiracy" has continued to broaden.

Just as the dust was settling on Home Secretary Theresa May's troubled review of historic sex abuse allegations – a second chairman, lawyer Fiona Woolf, had resigned over a potential conflict of interest – it emerged last week that one crime being investigated by the police was a "possible murder".

Last week, too, an official inquiry into the Home Office's handling of child sex abuse claims in the 1980s failed to uncover any of the missing documents that prompted the investigation."

Following on from the media's hidden agenda; it's almost as if "someone" sends out a message, that in turn goes throughout the entertainment industry grapevine; that they are to take every opportunity to besmirch and ridicule parties such as UKIP as much and as often as they can.

It seems an evening or weekend cannot go by without some programme or another, whether it be a quiz show like BBC-Have I Got News For You, BBC-Russell Howard's - Good News, or BBC-QI and where on the 27 February 2015 show, comedian Jack Whitehall had to jump on the bandwagon as perhaps he's the only one to date not to have had a dig at the UKIP party or Nigel Farage.

The show's host, Stephen Fry, introduced illustrations of some circus clowns with made-up faces; contestants are then invited to buzz-in with their opinions and say what the significance is and what comes to mind.

This is when comedian and self-acclaimed "posh-boy" - Jack Whitehall quips; "Clowns, err members of UKIP?" "They're clowns and frightening..." the audience respond with the expected laughter.

That's when fellow guest, Welsh comedian, Lloyd Langford, slipped in his one liner; "With their white faces..." and when more laughter pursued.

Meaning that UKIP was an all-white person party, full of clowns and quite frightening.

It would come as no surprise to learn the clown illustrations were shown specifically, (yes there are many set-up situations where the quests on many of these types of shows have rehearsed what they will say), so as they could make their joke about UKIP.

It was MP Kenneth Clarke who first accused UKIP as being "Clowns" and this was mentioned on BBC1 - Have I Got News for You - Series 45 Episode 5.

UKIP has members from all types of races. Take Croydon's Winston Mckenzie, he's a proud Blackman, ex-boxer and businessman. He served as UKIP's Commonwealth Spokesman from 2014 until 9th March, 2015.

Only a complete and downright ignorant idiot doesn't recognise that the vast majority of people within the UK are made up from one descendent or another and who originally came from somewhere else other than mainland Britain.

You're also as bigger a fool if you don't acknowledge that the "immigration problem" is purely because of the volumes involved and has nothing to do with nationality, race or creed.

For even if they were little green men from outer space, if there were millions of them wanting to land and settle here in the UK, we'd still have to say; "Nano-nano" and decline their wishes and until at least the infrastructure was put into place.

And until that time, they'd best stay-put and make the best of that world as opposed to another, that often enough the old adage; '...it's not always greener on the other side', is often proved to be the case.

For genuine asylum seekers fleeing war torn regions of the world, then of course their cases and argument is completely different than that of a financial-migrant and should be treated as so if proved to be the case.

As mentioned elsewhere, the British public have always been proud about the way they easily and tolerantly accept immigrants, especially those in need.

No one gets any pleasure closing the door on a genuine person whose only want and desire is to better their life.

Perhaps the only reason millions of people feel the need for such mass migration, is because their own countries governments are probably led by even more corrupt leaders than what there is currently here in the UK.

Knowing this is perhaps the key to solving their problems and maybe it's time for the populations around the UK, Europe and the world to rise-up and demand a better standard of living from their own 1%, leaders and government.

Lest you forget who, what and why your forefathers went to war in WWI and WWII.

The estimated death toll in World War II alone ranges from approximately 60 to over 80 million, making it the deadliest war in world history.

If the truth be known there are many among you who at one time in their lives would have never dreamed of voting for a political party such as UKIP.

Yet who perhaps now see them as being saviour's who could perhaps save the day and before it's too late for their country, - as opposed to being the racist ogres the opposition and mainstream media is in the habit of portraying them to be.

Though to be fair there have been some loose cannons acting like clowns and there are probably racist people within the party, yet it appears as soon as this comes to light they are soon expelled from the party.

Godfery Bloom's "Bongo Bongo land" comment, just made him look like a buffoon.

On 20 September 2013, UKIP withdrew the party whip from Bloom after its alleged he assaulted journalist Michael Crick in the street, threatened a second reporter, and at the party's conference jokingly referred to his female audience – as "sluts".

He didn't last long, nor would he gain many votes were he ever to stand as a candidate. He, and anyone like him are a disadvantage to UKIP and totally damaging to them. He left the party in October 2014.

Andre Lampitt, who appeared in a UKIP party political broadcast, was found out for holding what has been described as repugnant views.

Statements taken from his social media sites included; "Most Nigerians are generally bad people, I grew up in Africa and dare anyone to prove me wrong" and "Miliband is not a real Brit, I hope he never gets to be PM! He was only born here".

Again this is totally uncalled for, tarring "most" Nigerians with the same brush and no differently than someone saying all white people are racists.

After hearing what the Labour Party deliberately did in regards to immigration with their 'open-door' policy, letting millions flood into the country, is probably why someone like Lampitt holds such views.

There are many indigenous people who are extremely angry due to such a betrayal and rightly so.

Nonetheless, UKIP's first MP of Clacton, Douglas Carswell, says a "dislike of foreigners" is "offensive and absurd" and warns his party against making racist comments.

In a BBC fly-on-the-wall documentary, shown on the 22 February 2015, titled: 'Meet the Ukippers', footage of Rozanne Duncan, who sits on Thanet District Council, showed her saying she has a "problem" with "Negroes" - admitting she would refuse to attend dinner if seated next to black person.

Mrs Duncan said she felt "betrayed" after being expelled in December 2014 for bringing UKIP "into disrepute." But she has insisted she is not racist and does not regret what she said.

If anything, it just goes to show you how utterly

stupid she is and totally blind to her own racism, - or is she?

It's almost as if some of these UKIP members have deliberately infiltrated the party in the guise of trolling Trojan horses that pretend to be pro-the-party line, yet are clearly not and whose surreptitious comments are deliberately made so as to hinder and undermine it.

At the most sensitive of times and when world's media is shining their spotlights upon them, quoting and watching their every word and move, it seems they then muster-up the most damaging and controversial of sayings and comments they could possible come out with knowing full well it can only cause serious harm and damage to the party's reputation.

If it wasn't for a handful of people, perhaps some acting as spies-in-the-camp and trolls at the same time, the party would have probably gained even more support.

Nigel Farage has since repeated his condemnation of Mrs Duncan's remarks and stood by the decision to expel her from the party.

"Clearly she doesn't have any understanding of the deep offence she has caused by her comments, and we took the right decision," he told a BBC Radio 4's Broadcasting House programme.

Nigel Farage said "...the ordinary voters who are worried about immigration aren't racist."

He's right. When those voters look at people like ex-members such as Bill Etheridge, seen in the media holding a Golliwog, Godfrey Bloom, Andre Lampitt, Rozanne Duncan and others, and then take a good look at themselves in the mirror, they can see the difference.

Apart from suffering from bungling members that most parties have, it was announced on the 19 March 2015, that Janice Atkinson, MEP for the South East, had suspended; "following allegations of a serious financial nature", the party said.

She was due to fight the Folkestone and Hythe seat on 7 May, and this will of course hinder the party as not only is it embarrassing, it leaves them out on a limb to find the right candidate to replace her at such short notice.

At the time of going to print Ms Atkinson had not yet commented on her suspension, though a UKIP spokesman said; "...she appeared to have exercised poor judgement."

And that they are; "...incredibly disappointed with Ms Atkinson, who appeared to have acted in a way the party has never and would never condone."

He added: "The party has acted swiftly and immediately and just as we showed when we suspended another MEP for financial irregularities, we always maintain a zero-tolerance attitude towards acts of this nature."

In article by Miles Goslett 28 February 2014, in the Spectator magazine, it reads: "Over the last three years the BBC has secretly obtained millions of pounds in grants from the European Union.

Licence fee payers might assume that the Corporation would have been compelled to disclose the source of this money in its annual reports, but they bear no trace of it specifically.

In the latest set of accounts, for example, these funds are simply referred to as 'other grant income'.

Instead of making an open declaration, the BBC's successful lobbying for this money had to be prised out of it using a Freedom of Information (FoI) request lodged for The Spectator, proving that there was never any danger of the state broadcaster's bosses volunteering it willingly.

The FoI response confirms that BBC staff applied for, and accepted, about £3 million of EU funds between April 2011 and November 2013, most of which has been spent on unspecified 'research and development' projects, with the remaining £1 million spent on programming.

Next to the £3.65 billion tax-free income that the BBC receives each year via the licence fee, £3 million is, admittedly, a mere speck of dust – just 0.8 per cent of its annual guaranteed revenue and, obviously, even less than that when spread over 36 months.

However, the size of these EU gifts is arguably irrelevant, even though they are indicative of the BBC's seemingly unquenchable thirst for public money.

What is undeniably true is that the BBC has acted with characteristic slyness by concealing that it ever requested, let alone received, this European cash, suggesting that it is uneasy about the public being aware of its financial arrangements.

Rob Wilson MP, an aide to the Chancellor of the Exchequer George Osborne, says that he believes evidence of the BBC receiving any EU money leaves it open to attack because being on its payroll risks feeding the perception that is incapable of reporting objectively on European affairs.

Mr Wilson also questions why the BBC needed to go 'cap in hand' to the EU for funds in the first place when its enviably secure financial position allows it to outgun commercial rivals in so many spheres.

He says: "The whole point of the licence fee is to protect the BBC's political independence and impartiality by providing it with a source of funding that is outside the hands of governments and politicians."

Thanks to this FoI response, we now learn that it has been going cap in hand to the EU for millions of pounds on the quiet over the last few years.

Such outrageous flouting of the principles on which the BBC is based and funded will only promote cynicism about its political impartiality and lead to a loss of trust in the BBC's independence." - Miles Goslett.

Perhaps the time has come for UKIP or another political party, to announce they will also have a referendum on whether the BBC should be funded by the public or let them sink or swim against the other privatised channels.

We're sure there are millions of potential voters who would love to be given the opportunity to rid the country of such a propagandist gluttonous organisation - that on many levels is very much like the European Commission.

IMMIGRATION CENTRES

Nor was there any mention or comparison in Channel 4's First 100 Days of UKIP about the already appalling treatment of illegal immigrants when caught and then held in the private run immigration centres.

If anything else then perhaps UKIP could promise to carry-out and conduct a far better job of handling the present illegal immigration problem than that of today's coalition government.

According to a social media campaign known as "DetainedVoices", in support of inmates kept in detention centers such as the GEO run Harmondsworth immigration removal centre located near London's Heathrow Airport; poor conditions at the facility have forced nearly half of the inmates to go on hunger strike.

The strike had entered its seventh day on the 15th March 2015.

It seems due to the forthcoming General Election in May 2015, both the UK media and the British government are choosing to ignore this rather embarrassing fiasco.

So it's left to the likes of TV channels such as Russia Today who are more than willing to cover such humiliating exposés and where their reporter Harry Fear could be seen interviewing activists who were protesting outside the London detention center on 14 March 2015.

They demand that Harmondsworth and similar centres across the UK are shut down. "We've come here to fight to see that [the] detention centre is closed down and people are let free," one of the demonstrators, a Ugandan man named Ahmed, told RT.

Ahmed himself spent two months at Harmondsworth and claimed the conditions there are inhumane; "They lock people-up all the time.

There's no freedom.   There's no freedom of expression. The healthcare system is so unhuman," he said.

RT, along with independent journalists and human rights organisations, have collected stories from other inmates – all of whom echo Ahmed's words. "I've been detained for more than 17 months now and my friend – with me here – four years. I've seen everything. I've seen everything," one inmate said.

Harmondsworth "is like a prison," another detainee said, adding that "the conditions here are very bad. No one is allowed to go out. The officers working in here are very racist, behaving with us like we're animals."

Another man said he was worried about the fate of a fellow hunger striker who "went to hospital. He was vomiting because he wasn't eating. Now we don't know where he is."

The Guardian reported on the 16 March 2014; the chief inspector of prisons had accused Harmondsworth of a shocking loss of humanity after a terminally ill Canadian man was kept in handcuffs as he died in hospital.

Staff ignored a doctor's report declaring the 84-year-old unfit for detention or deportation and in need of social care.

The chief inspector, Nick Hardwick, said that on at least two occasion's staff at Harmondsworth immigration removal centre have needlessly handcuffed elderly, vulnerable and incapacitated detainees in what he called "an excessive and shocking manner."

He said that the two men were so ill that one died shortly after his handcuffs were removed and the other, the 84-year-old, who has been named as Alois Dvorzac, died while still restrained.

This kind of treatment in 2015, is not only cruel, it is utter madness; "17 months" or "four years" in other cases, shows us that the UK government have completely failed and have no real idea as to what to do to resolve this matter.

It seems they prefer to just lock-up illegal immigrants for an undetermined period of time rather than confront and sort out the problems full on.

Apart from being inhumane, these types of private run detention centers are costing the British tax payer billions of pounds each and every year.

That's why if the UK had full control of their borders, there would be no reason to have all these detention places in the first place.

It would be equally tragic were political parties such as UKIP, to keep such immoral institutions open and not introduce a fast-track solution.

It would be beneficial to all parties concerned that those who are currently held inside any detention centre to have the cases dealt with within weeks, rather than months or years and as fair and humanely as possible.

The "immigration problem" is not the fault of the 'immigrant' and why no vindictiveness, maliciousness or point scoring should be tolerated.

The main concern of the British public is the present open borders that being part of the EU brings with it.

We assume the first thing to achieve will be to close the borders and return to the old passport and visa system and not to let people in just using a national ID card.

That will be the telling factor of any party that is brave enough to tackle the immigration problem. That's why it is equally important and vital they get it right and that instead of 'militarising' the police and giving them and the border agencies carte-blanch in how they deal with such a sensitive issue and situation, it must be seen to be conducted in the most civilised and humanitarian way as possible.

As said throughout, the UK is made up of immigrants and from centuries ago.

No one, especially the British, who after all are made-up of all types of races, creeds and colours wants to see some type of Nazi jackboot thugs rounding-up and evicting "legal" (under EU law) or illegal immigrants and that whosoever job it is, they are trained to carry out their tasks in the most dignified of ways.

These people are not criminals for wanting to better their lives. Yet unfortunately there simply is not the infrastructure in place to cope with so many additional people.

The UK government need the powers to be able to curb the numbers entering the country and without being in breach of European legislation.

What's the alternative?

To let people continually arrive?

Of course not.

This is why Channel 4 and other biased programme makers are not helping to solve the matter at all.

In fact it's quite the opposite as people can see through the underline propaganda messages being sent out by them; which is anyone who questions, debates and wants to solve the immigration problem; is a racist.

When this is simply not true and that something has to be said and done to address this serious matter and problem and before it really is too late.

In many respects the experimental idea of a European Union transforming member state countries and regions across Europe into something more like that of the United States of America, that ultimately is part of the United Nations, (thus NATO & Agenda 21) established in 1945 to promote international co-operation and a replacement for the ineffective League of Nations;

thus eventually gathering all the nations from around the world and placing them under the umbrella of a single global supranational new world order government - sounds like a noble gesture and worthy cause;

if it could eradicate poverty, bring terrorism to an end and cease the need for nations to go to war, then this sounds like a wondrous utopian plan and world to live in.

If homelessness is addressed, the true nature and the issues of drugs and crime tackled, it opens up trade links and upholds the 'rights of man' in general, such as the right that every single person is protected from being exploited, abused, hurt or used in any disadvantageous way whatsoever by either corrupt governments or shady employers and that which then helps to enhance the lives of all those involved, then again of course it's certainly the right and benevolent way to go.

103

However, and here's the main problem; like most worthy ideas with the most gracious of intentions, there sadly always seems to be small or large groups or individual's hell bent on exploiting, corrupting and dominating the rest, which ultimately ends up destroying what originally was perhaps a virtuous conception and great idea.

A supranational worldwide government is far from being a new concept, time and time again history has shown such attempts.

Though no complete world government has ever existed throughout human history, there have been several empires or dictatorships that encompassed substantial portions of the then known world.

Famous examples are the Persian Empire, which Alexander the Great seized and claimed as his own empire, as well as the Roman Empire, the Mongol Empire and of course the British Empire.

In the case of the British, a quarter of the world's land surface and approximately a third of the world's population was part of that Empire. This is the single closest time that the world has ever come to a total political unification.

It's almost as if the German's still dwell and strive for such as empire and it could be argued with the European Union they are - or should we say, were almost successful in achieving it?

As noted previously, on the 17 March 2015, the world's population stood at 7,301,925,777.

According to a study by anti-poverty charity Oxfam, the wealthiest 1% will soon own more than the rest of the world's population combined.

The charity's research shows that the share of the world's wealth owned by the richest 1% increased from 44% in 2009 to 48% in 2014.

On current trends, Oxfam says it expects the wealthiest 1% to own more than 50% of the world's wealth by 2016.

The research coincided with the start of the 2015 World Economic Forum in Davos. The annual gathering attracts top political and business leaders from around the world whom all fall into this 1%.

Yet this leaves bit of a dilemma for the billions of us who remain outside the arena the 1% reside in, for those inside this elite Amphitheatre of life really do not view "everyone" as a collective, despite on the exterior they may give the impression that they do and that their long term plans and great visionary ideas are for the greater benefit of mankind; - the simple truth of the matter is, it is often not the case and the only ones who truly benefit, is themselves and no one else.

The same old people who stem from the already existing 1% and whose own countries have never yet been able to sort-out its own internal strife and political affair - and as we've just touch on; such as dealing with the distinctive inner-city problems of not having enough social housing, (1.8 million people are on the social housing lists in the UK alone).

The problems of drugs, poverty, crime and such high unemployment rates, despite the British government massaging the figures and proclaiming there is less unemployment than before, for as said elsewhere, the majority of people declared "unemployed" before the coalition government was forced upon the nation in 2010, have been taken off "unemployment benefits" and placed onto some other type of non-productive and equally as expensive schemes or universal credits.

The truth is they are being forced to become "self-employed" and work for Universal Credits and zero contract hours and purely because there are more people than there are actual vacancies available.

So knowing of and seeing all this going on around them; then why the hell are "they" trying to amalgamate and forcibly fuse together the world's problems and tackle them as one?

Of course people from other cultures can and do live in harmony, after all we all human beings who share the same type of inspirations, dreams and desires;

yet you cannot expect to force something upon others and especially if it's ill-conceived and thought out like that of the EU and benefiting just a minority.

Instead, why don't they at least try and address

and sort out their own backyard and wayward children before knocking on their neighbour's door and telling them how they should or shouldn't be raising theirs?

Nevertheless, in-spite of all the facts it's the same inept 1% of groups of people who have the nerve to envisage and demand a European Union along with their New World Order of a supranational worldwide government, - when all around us it's crumbling and tumbling down.

Though here's the hard facts and why you better start opening your eyes; for even though we say 'inept' – it's basically long been devised to function this way.

As it's all to do with the continuity of maintaining control and power.

"They" thrive by ruling and dividing the nations. Their objectives are not to promote and sustain racial and religious harmony, as it's deliberately contrived to provide a continuous conveyer-belt of slave workers for those 1%.

That's why wages are and always have been low - and for those fortunate enough to find employment the vast majority of them are being forced to live hand-to-mouth each and every day.

It's no different than being in an abusive relationship and why it's time to say enough is enough and to fight back and claim what is rightly yours.

In many respects the United Kingdom Independence Party (UKIP) is the prodigy of these former or existing number of groups and parties of Euro-sceptic's.

Get Britain Out (GBO), formerly known as the Anti-Common Market League (ACML), first established in 1961 in response to the failed attempt of those who wanted to get Britain to enter the European Economic Community (EEC) the previous year.

Led by John Paul and Michael Shay, the group was initially restricted to Conservative Party members.

Its President Victor Montagu, in Godfrey Bloom style also courted controversy when he claimed that the British did not want to be led by "a bunch of frogs and Huns", and very much like UKIP, the ACML soon distanced itself from xenophobia, whilst also opening membership to anyone regardless of their political party affiliation.

Under the chairmanship of Sir Robin Williams (1969 to 1984) the group became a constituent member of the National Referendum Campaign, an umbrella movement associated with The Spectator magazine.

It included a number of different groups; such as the British League of Rights, MP Ron Leighton's Get Britain Out, the Scottish National Party, Plaid Cymru and the United Ulster Unionist Party, as well as leading politicians such as Barbara Castle, Michael Foot and Enoch Powell.

It was following the demise of this broad coalition, the ACML continued to operate, being particularly vocal in its criticism of the Common Agricultural Policy and moves towards devolution, whilst campaigning for free trade with the world as a whole rather than just the European Union.

Under the chairmanship of Peter Dul and Presidency of Richard Body, the group worked closely with the Anti-Maastricht Alliance and the Campaign for an Independent Britain (CIB).

The ACML, now the Get Britain Out (GBO) is affiliated to the latter organisation and appoints two members to its National Committee.

GBO claim to be an independent, non-party, grassroots campaign to get Britain out of the European Union.

They want to take back control of the country from unaccountable bureaucrats in Brussels and for Great Britain to be a sovereign country once again.

According to GBO, the indirect cost to the UK for being a member of the EU is staggering £55 million per day, due to the red tape involved it is costing British businesses £120 billion per year.

They want to trade with Europe but not be governed by Europe. They want to work with European member states on important cross-border issues, whilst highlighting the EU is an expensive, undemocratic and out of touch body and Britain's interests are not best served by retaining its membership.

Research confirms a power struggle between members of ACML and those who went on the set-up the Campaign for an Independent Britain (CIB), in 1969, two years after the original Joining the Common Market or What the Treaty of Rome Means booklet was first published by Political Intelligence Publications Ltd, which dissolved in 1970.

ACML "disbanded" and as said, today is known as Get Britain Out.

The same type of power struggle happened with the leadership of UKIP, which was founded in 1993 by Alan Sked and other members of the cross-party Anti-Federalist League (AFL), a political party set up in November 1991 with the aim of fielding candidates opposed to the Maastricht Treaty.

It attracted a few members of the Eurosceptic wing of the Conservative Party, which was split on the European question after the pound was forced out of the European Exchange Rate Mechanism in 1992 and the struggle over ratification of the Maastricht Treaty.

UKIP candidates stood in the 1997 general election, but were overshadowed by James Goldsmith's Referendum Party. (The Referendum Party contested 547 seats.

In the 165 seats contested by both, the Referendum Party beat UKIP in all but two - Romsey and Glasgow Anniesland, the latter by just two votes.)

After the election, Sked resigned from the leadership and left the party because, he said, it contained members who "are racist and have been infected by the far-right" and was "doomed to remain on the political fringes."

However, Goldsmith died soon after the election and the Referendum Party was dissolved, with a resulting influx of new UKIP supporters.

The leadership election was then won by the millionaire businessman Michael Holmes, and in the 1999 elections to the European Parliament, UKIP gained three seats and 7% of the vote.

In that election, Nigel Farage (South East England), Jeffrey Titford (East of England) and Michael Holmes (South West England) were elected and the rest is history.

As said before; it seems more than coincidence that we are being told how great our economies are recovery in the same year when countries all around the world including Europe; the UK, Gibraltar, Spain and Turkey, with Israel further away, also holding their General Election's - as are many more countries carrying-out various types of political elections.

Turkey are wanting and trying to convince their electorate that things are swell in Europe and why they too should join.

In the 51st Association Council meeting in Brussels held in May 2013, the Turkish Prime Minister Ahmet Davutoğlu claimed that Turkey had aimed for membership for 50 years and would continue to do so.

The European Union has already spent billions of euros working with Turkey to help it move toward being able to become a member of the EU.

There are some who are concerned about Turkey's potential membership and for several reasons:

First, they are concerned that Turkey's culture and values are different from those of the European Union as a whole. They point out that Turkey's 99.8% Muslim population, is too different from Christian-based Europe.

The European Commission state that the EU is not a religion-based organisation, Turkey is a secular (a non-religion-based government) state, and that 12 million Muslims currently live throughout the European Union.

Nonetheless, the EU acknowledges that Turkey needs to "...substantially improve respect for the rights of non-Muslim religious communities to meet European standards."

Secondly, some point out that since Turkey is mostly not in Europe (neither population-wise nor geographically), it should not become part of the EU.

The European Commission states; "The EU is based more on values and political will than on rivers and mountains," and acknowledges that, "Geographers and historians have never agreed on the physical or natural borders of Europe."

A third reason is Turkey's non-recognition of Cyprus. To join the EU, Turkey will have to acknowledge Cyprus to be considered a contender for membership.

Additionally, many are concerned about the rights of Kurds in Turkey. The Kurdish people have limited human rights and there are accounts of genocidal activities that need to stop for Turkey to be considered for European Union membership.

Finally, some are concerned that Turkey's large population around 81,691,392 would alter the balance of power in the European Union. After all, Germany's population (the largest country in the EU) is only at 82 million and declining.

Turkey would be the second largest country (and perhaps eventually the largest with its much higher growth rate) in the EU and would have considerable influence in the European Union. This influence would be especially profound in the population-based European Parliament.

113

The low per-capita income of the Turkish population is also of concern since the economy of Turkey as a new EU member might have a negative effect on the EU as a whole.

Turkey is receiving considerable assistance from its European neighbours as well as from the EU. The EU has allocated billions and is expected to allocate billions of euros in funding for projects to help invest in a stronger Turkey that may one day become a member of the European Union.

According to a European Commission statement; "Europe needs a stable, democratic and more prosperous Turkey which adopts our values, our rule of law, and our common policies.

The accession perspective has already driven forward bold and significant reforms. If the rule of law and human rights are guaranteed throughout the country, Turkey can join the EU and thus become an even stronger bridge between civilisations as it is already today."

1 January 1973 and the UK joins the "Common Market" - European Economic Community (EEC). Negotiations were conducted by the then Tory Prime Minister, Edward Heath.

And ever since that day it seems as if they've been kicking the referendum ball around the place and avoiding the chance to score whenever it appears someone gets near the goalmouth.

It is almost to the day, when eleven years ago Tony Blair announced on 20 April 2004 that he would be holding a referendum, as he wants to 'let the people say' whether or not the UK should be in the centre of Europe or not.

There are many people, especially those too young to know or those too old to recall when in 1974, Labour, under the leadership of Harold Wilson, promised a referendum on whether to remain in the EEC in the party's election manifesto.

6 June 1975: The public endorse the UK's continued membership of the EEC, with 67% of people voting to stay in at a referendum, the question was:

"Do you think the UK should stay in the European Community (Common Market - EU)?"

And very much the same kind of 'in/out' question that will be put to them again were it ever to come about from the Conservatives and the other parties promising a referendum.

The "Yes" campaign was officially supported by Wilson's Government and the majority of his cabinet, including Denis Healey, the Chancellor of the Exchequer; James Callaghan, the Foreign Secretary; and Roy Jenkins, the Home Secretary.

It was also supported by the majority of the Conservative Party including its newly elected leader Margaret Thatcher, the Liberal Party, the Social Democratic and Labour Party, the Alliance Party of Northern Ireland and the Vanguard Unionist Progressive Party.

The "No" campaign included the left wing of the Labour Party, such as Tony Benn, Michael Foot, Peter Shore and Barbara Castle. Some Labour "No" supporters were on the right wing of the party, such as cabinet minister Eric Varley; though surprisingly you can see it's the "left" who were opposed remaining part of the EU and not the assumed far-right.

148 Labour MPs opposed their own government's measure, whereas only 138 supported it and 32 abstained.

Some members of the Conservative Party also supported the "No" campaign, although there were far fewer Eurosceptic figures in the Parliamentary

Conservative Party in 1975 than there would be during future debates on Europe, such as the accession to the Maastricht Treaty.

Most of the Ulster Unionist Party opposed the question, most prominently the former Conservative minister Enoch Powell, who was the second most prominent anti-Marketeer in the campaign.

Other parties supporting the "No" campaign included the Democratic Unionist Party, the Scottish National Party, Plaid Cymru and parties outside Parliament including the National Front and the Communist Party of Great Britain.

Just prior the referendum in 1975, the Labour government sent each UK household a printed leaflet and with a list of aims and beneficial reasons as to why the country should remain in the "Common Market".

(In brackets are our own comments and updates on the situation.)

The aims of the Common Market are:

• To bring together the peoples of Europe.

(Businesses, tourism and travelling, along with today's internet and with centuries of inter-racial marriages across many cultures and prior to joining the Common Market, have long brought together the peoples of Europe and the rest of the world.)

• To raise living standards and improve working conditions.

(It was reported on the BBC 11 October 2011 that middle-income families were set to see the biggest fall in their living standards since the 1970s, according to a new report. The Institute for Fiscal Studies estimates the stagnating economy will also push a further 600,000 children into poverty.

The situation in 2015 remains the same, with zero hour contracts, the working conditions are far worse.

Following the 2015 March Budget, the Chancellor of Exchequer George Osborne had the audacity to claim families were better-off today than they were in 2010 just following one of the worse recession to hit the planet, along with announcing a further £12bn cuts from welfare spending.

However according to Paul Johnston, of the Institute for Fiscal Studies, the Chancellor needs to spell out exactly how he plans to cut £12bn from welfare spending.

"Only £2bn of these £12bn cuts have been outlined so far. Yet all the cuts are supposed to be in place by 2017-18," he said.

Spending cuts planned for 2016-17 and 2017-18 would be "twice the size of any year's cuts over this parliament."

The Chancellor's hopes to raise a further £5bn in anti-tax avoidance measures, though if handled anything like the HSBC tax evasion scandal, it doesn't bode well.

Tax evasion by HSBC Bank for the 1% in Switzerland "is systemic and deep-rooted" says the Gas Workers and General Union (GMB).

Paul Kenny, GMB General Secretary, said; "This is another example of tax evasion on a massive scale that is endemic, systemic and deep rooted in the City and the wealthy classes across the country. This is criminal activity on an industrial scale.

Instead of tackling it the Tory Party has colluded in covering it up. The boss of the bank was promoted to be a minister in the Government. The credibility of this class in dealing with the deficit fairly has taken a very bad knock")

• To promote growth and boost world trade.

(That following on from the world recession of 2008/9 it was reported that world economic growth fell to just 0.5% in 2009, its lowest rate since World War II, warned the International Monetary Fund (IMF).

The IMF had predicted world output would increase by 2.2% in 2009.

It then projected the UK, which then entered recession, would see its economy shrink by 2.8% in 2010, the worst contraction among advanced nations.

20 January 2015 it was reported in the media that

119

the IMF sharply downgraded UK growth in 2014 to 2.6%, as every major economy in the EU falls short.

Britain's economy grew much less than predicted, the International Monetary Fund warned.

The global finance watchdog now thinks growth of just 2.6 per cent was achieved in 2014, compared to a previous forecast of 3.2 per cent.)

• To help the poorest regions of Europe and the rest of the world.

(Though it appears they can't even look after their own poor here in the UK, let alone in Europe.

When Labour came to power in 1997, according to the DWP, over a quarter of the UK's children - 3.4 million were living in poverty.

In 2006, David Cameron said he felt poverty was an "economic waste" and a "moral disgrace", then does nothing about it.

In 2014 child poverty here in the UK is worse than in Slovenia.

In a Unicef study of children's material well-being, measuring how little money and essentials they have, the UK came below other economies like France and Austria.

Two-thirds (66%) of children growing up in poverty live in a family where at least one member works, according to the Department for Work and Pensions (DWP) figures.

The figures went down to 2.7 million in the first two terms of Labour, jumping to 2.9 million in 2007/2008 as the banking crash hit, before slipping to 2.8 million in 2009.

Despite these type of salaries being paid to employees of charities and for decades, in February 2014 there was outrage over the £234,000 salary of the top boss of the Save the Children charity and where over 20 other charity chiefs earned over £100k pa.

The highest paid employee was at Marie Stopes and earned £290k.

In 2014, according to the Institute for Fiscal Studies, the coalition's reforms will increase absolute poverty in the UK by 400,000 in 2020.)

• To help maintain peace and freedom.

(Not to mention the wars in Iraq, when it was known no 'weapons of mass destruction' existed. Afghanistan, Syria, Libya, the middle-east and now in "Europe" in the war torn region of eastern Ukraine and where it is all too possible that the outline of World War III is taking shape and why there are calls for a European army.)

So continuing on the referendums question; since 2010, polls have indicated that the UK public is divided on the question whether to withdraw from the EU or remain with opposition peaking in November 2012 at 56% compared to 30% who wanted to remain and support peaking in 2013.

The largest ever poll (20,000) showed the public to be split on the issue, with 41% in favour of withdrawal, 41% in favour of membership, and 18% undecided.

However, when asked how they would vote if Britain renegotiates its terms with the EU, and the government says British interests are better protected, a wide majority of over 50% said they would vote to stay.

Though with the mass influx of illegal and "legal" immigrants flooding the EU and with many more deciding to head for the UK, it appears the horse has already bolted and why the British electorate seem to be changing their voting habits, opinions and ideas.

On the 17 July 2012, the Telegraph held a vote, the question was; "Would looser ties with Europe hinder UK trade?" - Yes - 14.05% (740 votes) - No - 85.95% (4,526 votes) = Total Votes: 5,266.

It went on to report: Companies have focused their efforts on fast-growing economies in Latin America and Asia, as they attempt to offset the effects of the downturn in the Eurozone, where demand for British-made goods is slowing.

Some 51% of British exports in the three months to May went to countries outside the EU, marking a

13.2% rise on the previous year, according to the Office for National Statistics (ONS).

By contrast, exports to countries within the EU fell by 7.2%, with the Eurozone's hardest hit countries seeing the biggest fall in demand. Exports to Italy fell almost 20% compared and have probably falling even more in the last two or three years, while exports to Portugal and Spain were down by 14.5% and 9.2% respectively and with further declines coming from these regions.

It is only due to the rise of UKIP that the British public have half-heartedly been promised a referendum by most of the political parties.

In January 2013, British Prime Minister David Cameron promised an "in/out" referendum on British membership of the European Union in 2017, though only after a period of renegotiation with the EU, if the Conservative Party wins the General Election with an outright majority on the 7th May 2015.

As said, this basically means this is very unlikely to ever happen as many political experts are again forecasting no outright majority and the likelihood of another collation government is on the cards.

Besides, there's no mention of a solution on how to tackle the immigration crisis that is getting more and more out of control by the day.

Both Labour and the Liberal Democrats oppose the policy of guaranteeing a referendum in 2017, holding instead that a referendum should only be held if there is a further transfer of sovereignty to the European Union;

that surely with the recent mention of a European army, which we cover in a moment, this does indeed further transfer sovereignty to the EU and therefore ups the-anti for a referendum to be called for.

As otherwise, what they are really saying, is no to even holding a referendum in the first place.

Then, like that of the Conservatives and after knowing what Labour deliberately did with Lord Mandelsons' admitting "they" were; '...sending out search parties for people and encouraging them - to take up work in this country,' - that back under their watch the immigration problem will only grow tenfold and in no time at all.

On the 15 March 2015, George Osborne refused to rule out a power-sharing deal with Ukip. It came as Mr Farage said he would be willing to support a Tory minority government only if a referendum on Britain leaving the EU was held before the end of 2015, two years earlier than David Cameron plans.

UKIP, in the 2013 county council elections across England, the party achieved its best ever local government result, polling an average of 23% in the wards where it stood, and returning 147 elected councilors.

It made significant gains in Norfolk, Lincolnshire and Kent, taking 15, 16 and 17 seats respectively. It was described as the best result for a party outside the big three in British politics since the Second World War.

In local elections in 2014, UKIP won 163 seats, an increase of 128, but did not take control of any council.

In European elections in March 2014, Ofcom awarded UKIP "major party status" for the 2014 European Elections, in England and Wales.

This gave UKIP the right to the same number of party election broadcasts as the three larger parties as well as having its views given "due weight" in broadcast news on ITV and Channel 5.

The BBC has since indicated that it will also do this.

Following weeks of refusing to appear on a live TV debate, on the 17 March, it was announced by the Conservative party, David Cameron has agreed to take part in a single TV debate in the run up to the election.

The proposed debate is to take place on April 2nd and will be a seven way face-off with Labour, the Lib Dems, UKIP, the Greens, the SNP and Plaid Cymru.

UKIP received the greatest number of votes (27.49%) of any British party in the 2014 European Parliament election and gained 11 extra MEPs from a total of 24.

The party won seats in every region of Great Britain, including its first in Scotland, which Farage called a "breakthrough."

It was the first time in over a century that a party other than Labour or Conservatives won the most votes in a UK-wide election.

Farage said; "...the result would change British politics fundamentally."

These results caused a political earthquake severely shaking the foundations of these latter quoted parties.

It is why it's claimed they too have jumped on the referendum bandwagon with David Cameron seeing this type of result on the horizon and why he decided to promise an 'in/out' referendum as the polls indicated that UKIP were about to win a landslide victory in the forthcoming UK local elections that took place on Thursday 2 May 2013.

Though it must be understood that despite these other political parties having to concede in giving the general public a 'referendum', they clearly have no intention of getting the UK out of the EU and why many of the British public have lost all faith in these other political parties and why UKIP are making some many gains.

Before the January 2013, Cameron had previously rejected a referendum on Britain's EU membership, but suggested the possibility of a future referendum to ensure the UK's position 'within an evolving EU' has the "full-hearted support of the British people".

Even though the Labour Party say they support a referendum, they do not at the current time, but have not ruled it out for the future.

The Liberal Democrats have said they do not support an 'in/out' referendum because it is within Britain's interests to remain a member.

Apart from UKIP wanting to hold a referendum this year, and the three main political parties promises and views on the matter; the Green Party, the Respect Party and the British National Party, all now support a referendum.

This appears to leave UKIP as the only credible party worth voting for if voters want to help stem the flow of immigrants, both "legal" and illegal from entering the country.

As they promise to leave the EU and restore power back to the UK.

They believe in 'free trade', though not political union with other European states.

The UK is the EU's largest export market, thus depend on the UK for jobs and not the other way around.

They state they will regain control of UK borders and of immigration, which will only be possible by leaving the EU.

Meanwhile and sensibly so, they wish to adopt the same kind of preconditions other countries like the USA or Australia have long had in force.

They insist before anyone is permitted to settle in the UK, immigrants must be able to financially support themselves and their dependents for five years.

This means private health insurance (except emergency medical care), private education and private housing, should be paid for and that within that time they would have paid into the tax system and become legible to receive the same full benefits as those others who have lived here for more than five years.

While no state has ever withdrawn from the EU, Greenland, part of the Danish Realm, voted to leave the EU's predecessor, the European Economic Community (EEC), in 1985, and Algeria left upon independence in 1962, having been a part of France until then.

The first United Kingdom European Communities membership referendum, 1975 endorsed the continuation of the UK's membership.

On the 6 January 2015 the Reykjavik Grapevine reported; 'Iceland is expected to withdraw its application to become a member of the European Union.

"Participating in EU talks isn't really valid anymore. Both due to changes in the European Union and because it's not in line with the policies of the ruling government to accept everything that the last government was willing to accept. Because of that, we're back at square one," Said Icelandic Prime Minister Sigmundur David Gunnlaugsson.

On the 27 February 2015 thousands rallied onto the streets of Reykjavik to demand a referendum outside the Icelandic National Parliament.

The government has been presented with a petition signed by nearly 29,000 people, constituting to 11.9 percent of registered voters.

The current government of Iceland which came to power in May 2104 is made up of the same two parties that were in power when the country was hit by the financial crisis in 2008.

According to Halldor Fannar Sigurgeirsson in Guardian-Liberty Voice, it is claimed; 'what is causing the protests now, is the parliament's consideration to cancel the negotiations to join the EU all together and possibly feeding on the simmering political atmosphere of the European economic region, as witnessed recently where an opposition in the Ukraine seeking to tighten the relations with the EU clashed with the Pro-Russian Prime Minister.

There seems to be a growing concern in the UK to leave the EU and Angela Merkel voiced her ideas to create a European internet to prevent digital espionage, as reported by whistle blowers, is to have been the case in Germany's deteriorating relationship with the United States.

A few weeks back, Non-EU trading partner, Switzerland, moved toward a direction to regulate the free flow of EU nationals through its labour market.'

Following the referendum of 1975, around 400 to 500 National Front members rallied against the UK's membership of the EU.

They were flanked by 2,000 police officers, having marched through north London protesting against the government's plans for immigrants to be able to enter the UK, and violence flared as other protestors demonstrated against the rally.

One demonstrator died, the first death at a demonstration in 55 years, and many protesters were injured, as were some police.

Police horses were used to clear a way through and a large number of arrests were made.

FINANCIAL SINKHOLES IN EU

On the 23 October 2012 - the European Commission agreed a series of demands that increased EU expenditure by £95 billion over the next eight years.

In response to this, the then Foreign Secretary

William Huge addressed MEPs saying; "People simply do not understand why there should be massive increases in the EU budget when all EU countries are trying to balance the books at home."

A staggering sinkhole of €3.5 trillion (£2.8trn) worth of more debt is now owed by EU member states, than when the last EU budget was negotiated.

David Cameron feebly tried to object, yet to no avail to veto a Brussels demand for over £80 billion in increases for the long-term EU budget running from 2014 to 2020 at a summit held in November 2012.

Rejecting the Prime Minister's call for a long-term spending freeze, the European Parliament and Commission also tabled demands for increased expenditure in 2012 and 2013. The Commission demanded a £7.3 billion spending increase by the end of year 2012 to meet a funding shortfall, figures that are disputed by Britain and other governments.

MEPs voted to reinstate over £6.5 billion in funding that had been cut by national government from the 2013 budget. The EU assembly also voted to support the commission's demand for an 11% increase in the "multi-annual financing framework" (MFF) for 2014-2020 while warning Mr Cameron not to attempt a veto.

Hannes Swoboda, the Austrian leader of the European Socialist Party, that includes Labour MEPs, sternly warned Mr Cameron that if he succeeded in cutting long-term spending – 'the EU parliament would use its own legal powers' to impose an even higher EU bill on British taxpayers.

"The UK taxpayer is being used as a cash cow by the EU said Nigel Farage. "The EU is one political club whose membership fee is becoming prohibitive," said Nigel Farage.

Many have ridiculously criticised UKIP for having MEPs in Europe if they are so anti the European Commission.

The world's austerity measures and recession had been forced on the public once again following the global financial crisis of 2007–2008, considered by many economists to have been the worst financial crisis since the Great Depression of the 1930s.

The crisis played a significant role in the failure of key businesses, declines in consumer wealth estimated in trillions of U.S. dollars, and a downturn in economic activity leading to the 2008–2012 global recession and contributing to the European sovereign-debt crisis.

The world has not yet recovered from this financial crisis and especially in Europe.

It's quite obvious why this post-recession obsession for austerity measures is being forced upon the nations of the world, as "they" need to make up for all those trillions of dollars, pounds and euros that had been totally wiped out in 2007-2008.

The huge bail-out bills to some members of the EU, is what spawned that derogatory term - the PIIGS of Europe, referring to the economies of Portugal, Italy, Ireland, Greece and Spain.

On the 19 March 2015, Greece's incredible debt was a staggering 443,866,382,489 euros, with an interest rate of 1,051 euros per second.

That equates to 40,251 euros debt per citizen and there's only 11,121,555, compared to the UK's population of 63,723, 120.

If you stacked-up Greece's debt in $1 dollar bills, the pile it would create would reach 32,033 miles high.

On 26 January 2015 - Alexis Tsipras and his radical anti-austerity Syriza party formed a coalition with the nationalist, populist, anti-austerity Independent Greeks (ANEL) to control 162 seats in the 300-seat parliament.

Alexis Tsipras, the Greek prime minister, has since threatened to leave the EU, and with Spain and Italy thinking along the same lines.

On the 4 March 2015, Greece's outspoken finance minister, Yanis Varoufakis, threatened to hold a referendum if the Greek government's reform programme was rejected.

With their Defence Minister Panos Kammenos going as far to say that Greece would then "flood" Europe with refugees, including potential Islamic State members.

Greece believes it's being sacrificed on the altar of the German austerity model, the EU Commission recently let influential EU members France and Italy off the hook again for not sticking to budget deficit rules.

It's been argued that their finances cannot be compared directly to Greece, but the incident served to heighten tensions, a feeling of injustice and suspicions of divergent visions inside the EU.

So serious is the situation in Greece, it could indeed and probably will have a domino effect.

This is why according to the Telegraph's journalist Andrew Lilico; discussions of what Greece might or might not get in the way of concessions from the Eurozone, there has so far been relatively little appreciation of one basic political reality, that as far as the PIIGS of Europe and perhaps even France are concerned, Syriza must fail - and must be seen to fail!

Germany wants Greece to arrive with a plan on the repayment of €328bn in bailout loans it received from the international community.

A special debt meeting followed by a summit of European leaders, the first with Alexis Tsipras on the 19th and 20th February 2015.

But a Greek government official ruled out accepting a plan based on the old bailout and said Greece would ask for a bridging loan to tide Athens over until it can present a new debt and reform program.

"We will not accept any deal which is not related to a new program," an official told the media.

Following the summit, Germany's Finance Minister Wolfgang Schaeuble told a meeting of conservative lawmakers on 26 February 2015, that recent remarks by the Yanis Varoufakis, the Greek finance minister, had strained European solidarity and that a bailout extension for Athens could be ditched if the country failed to stick to its promises, according to participants.

Wolfgang Schaeuble said of Yanis Varoufakis; "it strains the solidarity of European partners" - in interviews where he has resurrected talk of a debt haircut for Greece and cast doubt on its ability to repay its international debts.

Basically what's happening in the EU in regards to the financial crisis, is somewhat like watching a slow motion car crash.

Even if a "deal" is reached between Greece and their EU funders, it cannot last. Greece's debt and the repayment rates and conditions remain so high, something has to give.

Alexis Tsipras is walking on egg shells within his own country and in Europe.

He made promises that he probably will not be able to keep and it's very likely there will be a major uproar within his country if he has to make U-turn and do what it is the Germans demand from him.

Within days of the German parliament voting to approve the four-month bailout extension for Greece that was agreed on 24 February 2015 among foreign ministers of the 19 countries that use the euro currency and the bailout-supervising "troika."

Greek leftists were outraged by what they see as Alexis Tsipras backtracking on election promises to ease austerity measures.

Just two days later, on the 26 February 2015 protesters took to the streets of Athens, smashing shop and banks windows, torching cars, firing fireworks and hurling rocks at riot police.

And like said, if the PIIGS of Europe see renegotiations can be achieved, they'd be foolish to not try and do the same as Greece.

It's very likely we are witnessing the beginning of the end of the EU and how it presently stands with other countries populations wanting to opt out of the Eurozone and go it alone.

TROIKA

The Troika is made up of the European Commission (EC), the European Central Bank (ECB) and the International Monetary Fund (IMF).

As far back as May 2010, the EC and IMF agreed to bail out Greece. 110bn euros were designated, with 80bn euros coming from the EC.

More specifically, it comes directly from the member nations that use the euro - 16 countries at that time, and before Estonia joined on 1 January 2011.

The EC, headed by President Jose Manuel Barroso, consists of 27 commissioners and is tasked with the day-to-day business of implementing EU policies and spending EU funds. Though the EC's executive body is subservient to the member states.

Germany, being Europe's largest economy, and the one with the most cash to hand, is perceived as having, in effect, the final say on these bailouts.

Ideas backed by the EC, such as common debt for all the euro nations, dubbed Eurobonds - have struggled when entering the German domestic debate.

Germany's Wolfgang Schaeuble has recently poured cold water on the idea. Germany, though the most powerful member of the Eurozone, is one of 17 nations.

If any country fails to ratify the decisions they take collectively, the plan dies.

In the first Greek bailout, 30bn euros has come from the IMF, which was created at the conference at Bretton Woods in 1944 as a means to regulate trade between nations in the aftermath of the Great Depression and World War II.

The other pillar of this system is the World Bank.

The institution has historically lent money to countries that are in deep economic trouble - Mexico in the 1980s, for example, Mexico again in 1995, south-east Asia and Russia in the late 1990s and Argentina in 2001.

The fund's role has expanded in the aftermath of the global financial crisis that struck in 2008.

The IMF's members have agreed to increase the body's lending capacity, which has now been tripled to about $750bn.

The IMF has a complex system of voting rights, ensuring it remains dominated by the US and Europe. The US exerts a veto, for example.

It is currently undergoing a review of the voting structure, its biggest change since its founding. In practice, this means that emerging nations like China and Brazil are likely to get a bigger say.

The final member of the troika is the ECB, of the 17 nations that use the euro. In May 2010, the ECB started to buy Greek bonds in an effort to bring borrowing rates down and calm markets.

Since then, it has bought the bonds of all the countries whose yields have shot up on debt fears - Irish, Portuguese, Spanish, and Italian debt.

This infuriated German bankers, who have complained of indiscipline. It also means that the ECB is itself now exposed to any Eurozone default - indeed, the Germans have already agreed to recapitalise the ECB if there is a run on it.

Although the Eurozone rescue fund was created in the second Greek bailout, investors feel that it is already too small to take care of further deterioration in the market.

Taking in all the previous measures, the ECB has moved very far from its original mandate to target inflation - and many central bankers are not happy about that.

In September, Germany's Juergen Stark, the ECB chief economist, resigned amid speculation of conflicts within the bank over its bond-buying programme.

According to Andreas Theophanous, Professor of Political Economy and President of the Centre for European and International Affairs of the University of Nicosia; "There is no country in which the Troika could claim success. The austerity measures demanded by the EU, ECB and IMF remind this professor of a doctor's prescriptions only making the patient worse."

"And it could get worse for us all: the Troika policies cannot be sustained without further strains in the Eurozone and the EU as a whole."

"Participation in the Eurozone makes it difficult for a country to pursue discretionary policies to address a serious recession, as it has to stick to a tight deficit reduction plan. This leads to the deepening of the crisis with further cuts in public spending and increased taxes. In effect we have a situation of automatic destabilisers!"

"These policies in conjunction with a tight monetary policy lead to a vicious deflationary cycle. For the Eurozone to function, there must be a system of fiscal support by the centre, a philosophy that is currently missing."

As a matter of interest; Chinese companies are to invest in the next-generation UK nuclear power industry, beginning with the £14 billion Hinkley reactor now under construction in the country.

Britain has recently signed up to be a founder member of the Asian Infrastructure Investment Bank (AIIB), a $50 billion Chinese-led venture to fund projects across the Asia-Pacific region. What's more interesting to note is that considering the money being invested, can you imagine the profits they expect to create.

UK PROPERTY FARCE

It could be argued that pre the 2008/9 Global Financial Crisis, the Eurozone was doing pretty well along with the rest of the world.

Despite most laymen and women being able to see the inevitable subprime mortgage collapse coming and that coincided with the U.S. recession of

December 2007/2009, that in turn rippled across the Atlantic flooding the UK, Europe and then the rest of the world; many economic experts pathetically said no one could have predicted the severity of the crisis.

In addition to previous recessions, the current austerity measures and the real threat of WIII in Europe, the "next major crisis" to hit the UK/Europe/World property markets is not 'subprime mortgages' being loaned to high risk borrowers, but the simple fact is that the value of properties are a farce, as they have misleadingly been well overvalued.

The reason for this is that if the banks declared this was the fact, then all the trillions of pounds worth of mortgages, ("their assets" until the mortgages have been fully repaid), could arguably be halved, in many cases - by even more.

As far back as June 2011, Ray Boulger of mortgage broker John Charcol said; "The way mortgage providers of house price indices seasonally adjust their figures is a farce (or, seasonally adjusted, comedy)."

As an example Mr Boulger said the underlying figures from the indices show a small rise over the first five months of the year, 0.5pc for Halifax and 3.1pc for Nationwide, but then he points out the picture given by the seasonally adjusted figures can be far more gloomy.

Both mortgage providers use seasonally adjusted figures to smooth the variations in their figures and to account for the natural variations in prices driven by changes in buying patterns during the year. Both figures are based on mortgage valuations, rather than underlying selling prices.

Many houses in parts of the UK, especially in London, some properties such as ex-council homes and flats are being ludicrously over-valued. Hence why ridiculous mortgages are being loaned to those crazy enough to pay these hyper-inflated property prices.

January 2015 prices for the 'leasehold' of a two bedroom ex-council ground floor maisonette, on a pretty rough housing estate in Hackney, east London, is valued on 'rightmove.co.uk' website for £420,000, when in all reality it's not worth more than £50,000 in bricks and mortar, though arguably £150,000.

However, with millions of both "legal" and illegal immigrants in the country all desperately needing housing, is what helps the banks mask the real value of properties.

Often quoting; "It's the demand that drives the housing costs and the market determines the value."

And why again it's in the interest of the 1% to keep it that way, though it's inevitable the bubble will burst again.

As mentioned before, that even though in many

respects the EU may well have been a noble and worthy cause, it has since possibly been proven it really has not been worth all the billions, if not trillions of pounds in sterling and euros being paid by the British public and other countries populations for simply having the privilege to say they are united members.

Like as the people of Iceland have done - and now Greece, perhaps the time has come that the people within their own respected countries woke-up and demanded a much better deal.

A deal that doesn't keep protecting the wealth of the same 1%, but one that makes them full of pride being who they are and feeling fulfilled from wherever they come from and without feeling the need to have to flee their homelands and make a life for themselves elsewhere.

It's quite remarkable how the Yorkshire Television series; The New Statesman, starring Rik Mayall as Alan B'Stard, was bang-on the money as to how many MPs actually do perform and abuse their positions of power as the B'Stard character regularly portrayed.

The New Statesman was a British sitcom of the late 1980s and early 1990s satirising the Conservative government of the time.

It was written by Laurence Marks and Maurice Gran, based on an idea by Rik Mayall.

B'Stard is an overtly ambitious, selfish, greedy, dishonest, devious, lecherous, sadistic, self-serving ultra-right-wing Conservative backbencher.

It wouldn't be correct or fair to say all MPs are as crazed as B'Stard, yet it does seem many share similar traits to him and why the character was written that way, - and it can be safely assumed there are many other B'Stard's in government and all around the world.

It helps to be able to comprehend how this world really works; the "1%" work no differently than the very same conglomerates they own and who spend billions of pounds on years of research & development (R&D) on their inventions, ideas and patent applications.

This means before something is made public, months or years of R&D has first taken place.

The same applies to procurement deals and contracts. It takes at the very least many months, though at least some years to prepare a nation to actually go to war and especially a world-war.

Apart from the billions of pounds required for the military equipment and hardware required, you then have your soldiers and the logistics involved to move and position them and the military equipment into the right locations.

That within itself can take many months.

This means that despite what politicians may say "publically", - if it's a matter of "state security" and especially of war, then they are hardly going to give anything away to their potential enemy.

After all, it's the element of surprise that can often be the winning factor.

It's why "they" have annual meetings in places such as Davos and organisations like the Bilderberg group have their gatherings; for it is at these secret events the world affairs are discussed and decisions made as what to do next.

Don't forget, most career politicians, like "B'Stard", already are or soon become millionaires.

Tony Blair being a prime example.

That like dodgy stockbrokers exist and who indulge in insider-trading, bankers who can lower or hike-up the interest rates to suit themselves such as the Libor scandal - and politicians can earn millions of pounds by simply knowing what contracts and procurement deals are going to be awarded to whatever companies by buying shares in them, then the same must be said about war.

If it's something like an Ebola outbreak, then you'll be finding out what pharmaceutical companies produce the right vaccines or medicine and likely to be awarded the governments lucrative contracts.

If it's something like a war in Iraq, Europe or elsewhere in the world, then it's the military–industrial complex (MIC) of companies that you look into.

The MIC comprises the policy and monetary relationships which exist between legislators, national armed forces, and the arms industry that supports them.

These relationships include political contributions, political approval for military spending, lobbying to support bureaucracies, and oversight of the industry. It is often referred to - as the iron triangle.

Also, when it comes to "war", often the right hand doesn't know what the left is doing.

And don't expect a smart cookie such as David Cameron to endorse the European Commission's recent call for a European army, knowing they'd more than likely create an uproar when public spending and austerity measures are being imposed on the general public, - and days before his government is to announce the country's 2015 Budget on the 18 March 2015, and the General Election weeks later in May.

If you're are one of those people who has been conditioned into believing that being a member of the EU is a good thing and that it places Great Britain at an advantage by being there, then you're probably living in a quaint county hamlet and totally out of touch as to what is really taking place in the rest of the country, – including Europe;

a place that arguably is on the brink of WWIII and a total economic collapse is soon possible.

The world's economy still hasn't fully recovered from the worst economic crisis since the 1930's Great Recession.

Peculiarly, so perhaps we could assume it's a deliberate "coincidence" that coincides following a worldwide recession, - is that of a world war.

In 1913-1914 world production and income declined during this period and were not offset until the start of World War I increased demand.

Incidentally, the Federal Reserve Act was signed during this recession, creating the Federal Reserve System, the culmination of a sequence of events following the Panic of 1907.

1929-33 – The Great Recession: Stock markets crashed worldwide. A banking collapse took place in the United States and spread worldwide.

The United States remained in a depression until the outbreak of World War II. In 1936, unemployment fell to 16.9%, but later returned to 19% in 1938 (near 1933 levels).

Yet that these figures are nowhere as bad as some European counties; 2014 unemployment figures; Greece 25.8%, Spain 23.7%, others not as bad, Italy 12.9%, yet Kosovo, not yet part of the EU, is 45.3%.

It's recently been seen and discussed in most of the world's media; a report released 2 March 2015, conducted by the European Leadership Network (ELN), predicts one of NATO's main contributors Britain, will likely drop their 2015-16 defence budget to 1.88 percent of UK GDP.

This was said to have come as a bombshell for some of the West's military elite.

With the head of the US army, General Raymond Odierno, telling the Telegraph, he was "very concerned" about Britain's possible defense cuts.

He warned that; "...while the US was willing to provide leadership in tackling future threats, such as Russia and ISIS [the Islamic State, aka IS or ISIL], it was essential that allies such as Britain played their part."

In contrast to Britain, Russia reportedly plans to increase its military spending by 33 percent in 2015-16.

British MPs warn the challenge posed by Russian President Vladimir Putin's assertive foreign policy, and the threat of Islamic State have bred the "most dangerous" global climate since the mid-1990s.

Former MI6 chief, Sir John Sawers, called for a rise in defence spending, also mentioning the "threat" coming out of Russia "not necessarily directly to the UK, but to countries around its periphery."

"The level of threat posed by Moscow has increased and we have to be prepared to take the defensive measures necessary to defend ourselves, defend our allies - which now extend as far as the Baltic States and Central Europe," Sawers said, according to the Guardian.

In turn, Moscow said it will take all "necessary measures" including military, technical and political to neutralise a possible threat from NATO presence in Eastern Europe, Russia's ambassador to NATO, Aleksandr Grushko, told the Rossiya 24 TV channel on 23 February 2015.

He added NATO's actions "significantly impair regional and European security, and pose risks to our security."

Grushko said NATO has intensified its military drills in Eastern Europe, with about 200 exercises in its eastern member states, mostly in the Baltic and Black seas, Poland and Baltic states.

According to RT news, Germany does not feel like increasing the military budget at any cost. Minister of Finance, Wolfgang Schäuble, has recently agreed there was a need to spend more on defense, but said that Berlin was not going to do it at least before 2017, Bild am Sonntag reported.

Though as suggested, is the British governments defence cuts announcement a cunning pre-election ploy, knowing full well there are many potential voters who are anti-war and would even go as far as scrapping Trident, saving billions of pounds of British taxpayers money each and every year, than rather face years of austerity measures.

So what "they" can cleverly do is pretend all is ok on the Eastern front, so much so, "they" are even prepared to slash the annual defence budget.

And that sometime after the general election or when the time is right, win or lose, "they" can then drop the real bombshell, - and once again pretend to you how their experts had no idea of the seriousness of the threat coming from that once clear Eastern front, and that it is only now the country has to beef-up its defence budget by 30% or more!

On the outside and the peripheral of Europe is where the UK is better-of placed. An independent island, not locked-in land mass that it seems to have now become.

The UK needs to be able to overlook and see what's truly happening on the horizon and make its own self-determining predictions and decisions beneficial to the people of Britain, as opposed to the current disadvantageous decision making that's being taken by an unelected body of bureaucrats comfortably sat in Brussels, for as each day goes by Europe is on the brink of WWIII.

"WAG THE DOG" - WAR

So with these additional dilemmas to hit the regions of the Europe and much worse than any financial crisis or its austerity measures; there's a serious threat of WWIII looming upon the horizon following Ukraine's 2014 coup d'état, and something we should all be concerned about.

As already mentioned, it appears that Greece will not be able to escape the austerity measures and stranglehold of the EU, despite being given a four month lifeline in February 2015.

Though when June 2015 comes around nothing would have really changed in Greece and they'll be back to square one and in more debt than ever.

It's the masses whom governments fear. For it is them who ultimately votes in the next leader and government or take matters into their own hands and as displayed in Independence Square in Kiev.

"They" know the austerity measures inflicted on the deprived populations of Europe are unsustainable and therefore the whole of the EU, and especially those member states such as the PIIGS, are sitting on a powder-keg of explosives and no one knows when it may explode.

"They", other European leaders have seen how many of the politicians were treated in Ukraine; beaten, shot, slapped about, murdered, dragged from behind their desks and down to the streets and thrown into dustbins, then covered in eggs, flour or paint.

Many European politicians are without doubt very concerned over their own safety and what their "own people" may do to them if they have to continuously announce more debt being imposed on the country along with austerity measures and no chance of jobs or a better standard of living is on the table, that full scale rioting and protests are but a hairs breadth away.

So in order to try and prevent the inevitable explosion it's in all "their" interests to destabilise Europe even more and by sending "their" nations to a 'wag-the-dog' war.

"War's" are a far more easier excuse to come up with than trying to justify where all the trillions of pounds or euros have gone missing from their countries public purses and why they owe so much money - and to who they owe it to – the 1%.

Wag-the-dog wars are ideal scapegoats as they permit them from having to defend and explain all their incompetence and deliberate failings that many politicians around the world have too financially benefitted from.

Not only from the banking financial crises, but from the numerous wars they regularly endorse and get their countries involved in.

And like with what has already been explained; they get to know all about the procurement deals and multimillion pound contracts that their governments will be investing in and long before it becomes public knowledge.

On the 24th February 2015, in the Guardian it read; "Britain was pulled closer towards a renewed cold war with Russia when David Cameron announced UK military trainers are to be deployed to help Ukraine forces stave off further Russian backed incursions into its sovereign territory."

Two weeks later on the 9 March 2015, European Commission President Jean-Claude Juncker, calls for a European army.

On the 17 March 2015, addressing a media conference, Russia's Foreign Minister Sergey Lavrov, accused the US of inciting Kiev to end the crisis in eastern Ukraine by force - by supporting the recent Ukrainian law on the special self-governing status of Donbass.

He said; "If Washington welcomes the action, which undermines the Minsk-2 deal/agreements, then we can only conclude that Washington is inciting Kiev to resolve the issue by military means."

153

Let's not forget what first took place in Ukraine - which all started over the question of 'national debt' and austerity measures.

Viktor Yanukovych, was the democratically elected president, in November 2013 and like most European countries and the rest of the world, Ukraine too suffered from corruption, mismanagement, lack of economic growth and a currency devaluation following the world financial crisis.

The Orange Revolution of late 2004 improved Ukraine's prospects of entering the EU; it was Viktor Yushchenko who hinted that he would press the EU for deeper ties and described a four-point plan: acknowledgment of Ukraine as a market economy, entry in the World Trade Organisation, associate membership in the European Union, and, finally, full membership.

Viktor Yushchenko asked Brussels mid-December 2004 for a clearer indication of Ukraine's prospects for membership, saying that; "The approved Action Plan reflects only the level of Ukraine-EU relations that we could have reached before the presidential elections in 2004."

Ironically, in 2012 the EU initialed deals on free trade and political association with Ukraine;

however, EU leaders stated that these agreements would not be ratified unless Ukraine addresses concerns over a "stark deterioration of democracy and the rule of law", including the imprisonment of Yulia Tymoshenko and Yuriy Lutsenko in 2011 and 2012.

Despite all this, Ukraine, is still not a member state of the EU, and like many other European countries, their cupboards were bare and too in need of a financial bailout.

This is when Viktor Yanukovych sees the Troika as a way to getting the funds the country needed. This would have established closer relations with the EU.

Ukraine has long been seen as an important but difficult political partner of the European Union.

According to some observers, this is due to certain factors; such as the unwillingness of the EU to expand into post-Soviet space, poor performance of the Ukrainian economy, lack of democracy (during the 1990's) and internal instability (following the Orange Revolution).

Also, some "experts" acknowledge the importance of the Russian factor in Ukraine-EU relations.

Ukraine's desire to join the European institutions dates back to 1994 when the government declared that integration to the EU is the main foreign policy objective.

In reality, little was done since Kiev had to take into account Russia, which remained its major trade partner and natural gas and fossil energy supplier.

So it appears the EU/Ukraine/Russian pact and question has long been in the making and was a matter of time before something was about to give.

Though, and what the EU has become famous for, which is their love of control and austerity measures, there was an association agreement with the European Union which would provide Ukraine with the funds it required, but depending to reforms in almost all aspects of Ukrainian society – including austerity measures.

At first the Ukrainian leader was going to accept the contingencies, but subsequently Russia offered them a far better financial deal, so Yanukovych ultimately refused to sign-up with the EU and signed a treaty and multi-billion dollar loan with Russia instead.

This obviously put a few noses out of joint and why it's alleged 'outside' interference came into play that led to protests and the occupation of Kiev's Independence Square.

In January 2014, this developed into deadly clashes in the square and in other areas across Ukraine, as Ukrainian citizens confronted the Berkut and other special police units.

The following month, Ukraine appeared to be on the brink of civil war, as violent clashes between protesters and special police forces led to many deaths and injuries.

On 21 February 2014, Yanukovych claimed that, after lengthy discussions, he had reached an agreement with the opposition.

However, later that day, he fled the capital for Kharkiv, travelling next to the Crimea, and eventually to exile in southern Russia.

On 22 February, the Ukrainian parliament voted to remove him from his post, on the grounds that he was unable to fulfil his duties, although the legislative removal lacked the number of votes required by Ukraine's then-current constitution.

Parliament set the 25 May 2014 as the date for the special election to select his replacement, then on the 24 February 2014 issued a warrant for his arrest, accusing him of "mass killing of civilians."

Yanukovych, still declares himself to remain "the legitimate head of the Ukrainian state elected in a free vote by Ukrainian citizens," and if we are to accept democracy for what it is, then surely this is still the case.

Russian President Vladimir Putin announced on 1 March 2014, a week after Mr Yanukovych was overthrown, that Moscow has the right to take military action in Ukraine to protect Russian speakers. This has created the biggest confrontation between Moscow and the West since the Cold War.

According to Ewen MacAskill, in the Guardian 5 March 2014; "A leaked phone call between the EU foreign affairs chief Catherine Ashton and Estonian foreign minister Urmas Paet revealed that the two discussed a conspiracy theory that blamed the killing of civilian protesters in the Ukrainian capital, Kiev, on the opposition rather than the ousted government."

In an 11-minute conversation which was posted on YouTube – it revealed that telephone calls between western diplomats discussing the crisis and shootings in Ukraine had been bugged.

In the call, Urmas Paet said; "...he had been told snipers responsible for killing police and civilians in Kiev were protest movement provocateurs rather than supporters of then-president Viktor Yanukovych." - Catherine Ashton responds: "I didn't know ... Gosh."

The leak came a day after Vladimir Putin, said the snipers may have been opposition provocateurs.

During the conversation, Paet is quoting a woman named Olga, Russian media identified her as Olga Bogomolets, a doctor – blaming snipers from the opposition shooting the protesters.

"What was quite disturbing, this same Olga told that, well, all the evidence shows that people who were killed by snipers from both sides, among policemen and people from the streets, that they were the same snipers killing people from both sides," Paet said.

He continued; "So she also showed me some photos, she said that as medical doctor, she can say it is the 'same handwriting', the 'same type of bullets', and it's really disturbing that now the new coalition, that they don't want to investigate what exactly happened."

"So there is a stronger and stronger understanding, that behind the snipers it was not Yanukovych, it was somebody from the new coalition," Paet says.

As recent as February 2015 and with Greece's newly elected Alexis Tsipras, threatening to veto sanctions, EU foreign ministers recently gathered in Brussels for an emergency meeting over Russia's alleged actions in Ukraine.

The session had been prompted by a bloody surge in vicious fighting around the eastern Ukrainian seaport of Mariupol, where a rocket attack killed 30 people on the 25 January 2015.

It is the latest escalation of a bloody conflict that has seen an estimated 5,300 murdered as separatists and Ukrainian nationalists contest territory. The Ukrainian government has consistently alleged Russian backing of the separatist movement – a charge strongly denied by the Kremlin.

And still the irony continues; as one of the alleged reasons the Treaty of Rome was first formed was so that it would make it impossible for European countries to go to war again.

Yet those sensing this major shift of discontentment simmering away in Europe, - and whose interest it is in and by hook-or-by-crook to keep the EU intact and no matter what it takes;

is it conceivable dark-forces could be at play?

Is there some kind of diversion tactics being deployed that will help dim the spotlight and take away all the attention from those complaining about the severity of the austerity measures being forced upon their nations, - that are on the brink of revolution?

We have to question; are EU "leaders" being coerced into having to think of much more dangerous adversaries such Ukraine and "the Russians are coming" on one front and "ISIS" on another with its newly born Islamic state in Iraq and Syria, - than rather think about and address the financial problems their countries are facing?

For it appears "someone" has pulled out of a hat a series of distractions; as according to news reports ISIS has a growing number of franchises in other Mediterranean states, a point not only underlined by the recent alleged terrorist attacks in Paris, where it's claimed on the 7 January 2105 - 12 people were killed during the Charlie Hebdo shootings in Paris.

On the 15 February 2015 Denmark was on high alert and a massive manhunt was under way after a man sprayed bullets at a Copenhagen cafe hosting a debate on freedom of speech and blasphemy, killing one person and wounding three police officers.

Hours after the cafe attack, further shots were fired at a Copenhagen synagogue. Two police officers were wounded by gunfire and a civilian was shot multiple times in the head. "We feel certain now that it was a politically motivated attack, and thereby it was a terrorist attack," Prime Minister Helle Thorning-Schmidt told journalists, close to the site of the first incident.

On the 28 February 2015, a leading Russian opposition politician, former Deputy Prime Minister Boris Nemtsov, was shot dead in Moscow by unidentified attacker/s in a car. He died hours after appealing for support for a march on Sunday 1 March 2015 in Moscow, against the war in Ukraine and the growing economic crisis in this country.

Russia's President Vladimir Putin has condemned the murder. Investigators said it could have been "a provocation aimed at destabilising the country."

Ukrainian President Petro Poroshenko described Mr Nemtsov as a "bridge between Ukraine and Russia." "The murderer's shot has destroyed it. I think it is not by accident," he said in a statement published on his administration's Facebook page.

The investigative committee said in a statement, that several motives for the killing were being considered including "Islamic extremism", as

Nemstov has spoken out about the Charlie Hebdo murders.

A lawyer for Mr Nemtsov reported that he had received death threats over social media in recent months; but for now there's only speculation as to why he was targeted. He openly opposed Moscow's role in the crisis in Ukraine - and the annexation by Russia of Crimea.

Mr Nemtsov was shot at around 23:40 (20:40 GMT) while crossing Bolshoy Moskvoretsky Bridge within a spitting distance of St Basil's Cathedral and the Kremlin.

Though you would have assumed a far less obvious location would have been preferred, so as to take the clear indication of guilt away from Putin. The assassin/s might as well have done it outside Putin's own personal residence.

It was alleged he was shot four times with a pistol. The alleged killers then jumped into a white car which then fled the scene.

Many of the West's media are pointing the finger of blame at Vladimir Putin, though it seems far too convenient for our liking.

There's the old saying; "...don't defecate on your own doorstep."

Besides, knowing there would be such a backlash and accusation, why would you make such a public display of his murder, when there's so many other ways the kill someone so as it looks like an accident.

At least it keeps everyone guessing if they still don't believe they died that way.

It's almost like some kind of contract killing so as the finger of blame would obviously be pointed at Putin and it has been.

It was reported in the media on 12 March that five Chechens, had been arrested and confessed to shooting Boris Nemtsov on the 5 March 2015.

It's been alleged they were most likely forced to confess under duress and tortured during detention.

After visiting the three of the Chechens, who were imprisoned in Lefortovo Prison in Moscow, Andrei Babushkin, a rights activist, said that the men had suffered multiple injuries after their arrest.

In a summary of the visit posted on the council's website, Mr Babushkin also reported that Mr Rustam arrested at the same time as the main suspect Zaur Dadayev, had disappeared and said he had asked Russia's Federal Security Service, previously the KGB, to account for his whereabouts.

According to Mr Babushkin, Mr Dadayev, previously a lieutenant in the Interior Ministry's forces in Chechnya and decorated for bravery, said that Mr Rustam was his former subordinate and that he had confessed to killing Mr Nemtsov because he was told Mr Rustam would be released unharmed if he did.

Mr Dadayev and Mr Gubashev, were both

charged with murder, and ordered to be jailed until April 28.

The other three suspects were not formally charged but were jailed pending further investigation.

Who can say for sure what's happened here, other than someone carried out the murder, and either the accused was setup and informed on after their involvement or they're being framed.

According to News reports on the 19 March 2015, ISIS has apparently claimed responsibility for a deadly terrorist attack on the 18 March at the Bardo museum in the heart of that country's capital in Tunis, Tunisia.

In an alleged audio statement posted online; "ISIS" identified two men Abu Zakariya al-Tunisi and Abu Anas al-Tunisi and thought to be the two gunmen killed during the attack.

It said they used "automatic weapons and hand grenades" to kill and injure what it called "crusaders and apostates" in the attack.

Tunisian Health Minister Said Aidi said 23 people are believed to have been killed, including at least one British women, 57 year old Sally Adey.

And that bloodshed, the ISIS message warned; "...this is just the start."

Tunisian authorities claimed there have already arrested nine people in connection with the attack, including four directly linked to the bloodshed, according to a statement from Tunisian President Beji Caid Essebsi.

NATO's – EUROPEAN ARMY

As previously mentioned; on the 9 March 2015, the European Commission President Jean-Claude Juncker called for the creation of a European army to face up to Russia and "other" threats and, assume ISIS is one of these.

He said such an army would restore the European Union's foreign policy standing and show it is serious about defending its values.

"Juncker", being the President, is showing the European Commission's true colours.

Previously the question of defence was a national responsibility of each EU member state.

If anything, Juncker reveals yet again how the sovereignty of each member state is being compromised by such a proposal and perhaps how close the EU really is to the USA and the North Atlantic Treaty Organisation (NATO).

Technically speaking there is no need for an additional European Army, due to NATO.

The North Atlantic Treaty, was signed in Washington, D.C. on 4 April 1949. The treaty established NATO.

The treaty was drafted by a committee in clandestine talks in Washington which was chaired by Theodore Achilles.

Earlier secret talks had been held at the Pentagon between 22 March and 1 April 1948, of which Achilles said: "The talks lasted about two weeks and by the time they finished, it had been secretly agreed that there would be a treaty, and I had a draft of one in the bottom drawer of my safe. It was never shown to anyone except John [Hickerson]."

(In 1940, Hickerson became secretary of the American section of the newly formed Permanent Joint Board on Defence. He held this position for the duration of World War II.)

"I wish I had kept it, but when I left the Department in 1950, I dutifully left it in the safe and I have never been able to trace it in the archives. It drew heavily on the Rio Treaty, and a bit of the Brussels Treaty, which had not yet been signed, but of which we were being kept heavily supplied with drafts.

The eventual North Atlantic Treaty had the general form, and a good bit of the language of my first draft, but with a number of important differences."

According to Achilles, another important author of the treaty was John D. Hickerson: "More than any human being Jack was responsible for the nature, content, and form of the Treaty..." – "It was a one-man Hickerson treaty."

The treaty was created with an armed attack by the Soviet Union against Western Europe in mind, but the mutual self-defence clause was never invoked during the Cold War.

Rather, it was invoked for the first time in 2001 in response to the 11 September 2001 attacks against the World Trade Center and The Pentagon in Operation Eagle Assist.

Mr Juncker has voiced support for a European army before, but he suggested Russia's military action in Ukraine had made the case much more compelling.

"With its own army, Europe could react more credibly to the threat to peace in a member state or in a neighbouring state," he said in an interview with German newspaper Die Welt.

If you look at what really took place in Ukraine, and as shown elsewhere in this book, Russia hasn't been a threat to peace in a member state of Europe.

The term "neighbouring state", which Ukraine is, though not a "member state", and seems to dismiss that's exactly what Russia is as well, as is Belarus a landlocked country in Eastern Europe bordered by Russia to the northeast, Ukraine to the south, Poland to the west, and Lithuania and Latvia to the northwest. The capital of Belarus is Minsk.

President Jean-Claude Juncker states that an European army will not be in competition to NATO.

Which of course is 100% correct as out of the 28 member countries of NATO, 25 are also EU member states, the other three are located in North America (Canada and the United States) and Turkey is in Eurasia.

The objective of NATO is that if an armed attack occurs against one of the member states, it should be considered an attack against all members, and other members shall assist the attacked member, with armed forces if necessary.

It could be further argued that due to the USA being accused as the major interfering force within Ukraine and that they are wishing to expand NATO within the region and the borders of Russia, is the main reason a so called European army has been called for by Juncker, as it permits the USA (NATO) to distance themselves from "European conflicts", when the 'same hand writing' is already there and that NATO is up to their neck in it.

It's very likely what we are witnessing in Ukraine, will soon start to erupt in Belarus, who in 2000 signed a treaty for greater cooperation with Russia, though it would be in NATO's interest if it were to follow the same footsteps of Ukraine, as they are the final piece in the jigsaw that fits snugly along Russia's border.

Somewhat like the people of Ukraine, over 70% of Belarus's population of 9.49 million resides in urban areas. More than 80% of the population is ethnic Belarusian, with sizable minorities of Russians, Poles and Ukrainians. Since a referendum in 1995, the country has had two official languages: Belarusian and Russian.

Juncker continued to say; "...a common European army would convey a clear message to Russia that we are serious about defending our European values."

It's this type of insistence that seems to confirm he has been "instructed" to say this as it seems to suggest there is no need for NATO, thus the USA are not interfering in the regions.

And why Mr Juncker argued; "...that the inter-governmental force NATO was not enough because not all members of the transatlantic defence alliance are in the EU."

This just means USA, Canada and Turkey are not part of "Europe", with the red carpet being rolled out for Turkey to join as soon as they can arrange their membership.

Juncker continues; "...a common EU army would send important signals to the world and the purchase of military equipment would "bring significant savings."

This is surely a false and incorrect a statement, for it already costs each individual member of the EU billions of dollars to be members of NATO, so to have an additional armed force can only mean additional costs; and why Juncker cleverly uses the term; "significant savings".

This just mean whenever "they" spend more on arms they will make "significant savings" on bulk discounts and no different than a 'Buy one – get one free' kind of promotion you can see in your local supermarket.

Yet all this retroact and these types of messages send out is in total contrast to what the Treaty of Rome was designed for, which was to; "...help reconstruct the economies of the European continent, prevent war in Europe and ensure a lasting peace."

That for Europe and the world to restart an arms race, it inevitably will lead to another world war.

As mentioned elsewhere, following a world recession, "war" soon comes into play.

With all the military equipment, soldiers and arms that are required to fight such enormous wars, costing trillions of pounds, euros, dollars and rubles, it will certainly soon help to kick-start the worlds stagnant economies.

Silencing the millions of people currently protesting and suffering from all the austerity measures being inflicted on them - and by the very same people who are suggesting they now go to war instead.

The 28-nation EU already has battle groups that are manned on a rotational basis and meant to be available as a rapid reaction force.

That thankfully they have never been used in a real-war crisis.

EU leaders have said they want to boost the common security policy by improving rapid response capabilities.

As "they" have done in the UK, Europe and the rest of the world, which is privatise almost every commodity, resource and major service; oil, gas, electric, water, transportation, metals and gems - that in turn earn billions of pounds in profits each and every year and in favour of shareholders and the 1%, yet at the detriment of the masses, is what the "conflict of interests" are really all about and what leads to world wars.

Capitalism, in its current form has proven it makes the 1% richer and the masses poorer.

"Communism/Socialism" in their present form and described perfectly well in George Orwell's –

Animal Farm, proves it's "corrupt" and greedy leaders who make such noble ideas fail.

The capitalists viewpoint and angle prefers to blame "human-nature" being at fault and thus its own downfall.

When the truth of the matter is, neither capitalism nor socialism have ever been able to freely operate without corruption and the interference from the 1% who always prosper and no matter what the politics are within the world.

This can only be achieved with "their" armies to threaten a weaker "enemy" and keep "them" in power and control.

It was also skillfully reported on the 9 March 2015 that a UK government spokesman said: "Our position is crystal clear that defence is a national, not an EU responsibility and that there is no prospect of that position changing and no prospect of a European army."

Though going back to what was referred to at the beginning of this chapter; in a world of cloaks, daggers and smokescreens; "they" often portray countries such as Britain, along with France as having been against and wary-of a bigger military role for the EU, allegedly fearing it could undermine NATO.

Yet that's more likely part of the devious game of war. Only a fool doesn't know it's the USA that "runs this town" - the world - and that Britain, including France, have long shared the same pocket.

It was the French who gave them the Statue of Liberty and the only three countries to share Cleopatra's Needle, the popular name for each of three Ancient Egyptian obelisks re-erected in London, Paris, and New York City.

So like that of the USA preferring to not be openly seen interfering in Europe with NATO. Britain and France like to not be seen endorsing ideas such as an European army; - though all these parties involved are the same main players behind NATO.

The Treaty of Brussels, was signed on 17 March 1948 by France and the United Kingdom, along with Belgium, the Netherlands and Luxembourg, and is considered the precursor to the NATO agreement of 1949.

We now know NATO was established prior to Great Britain and France signing the North Atlantic Treaty, with Theodore Achilles confession confirming; 'earlier secret talks had been held at the Pentagon between 22 March (just 3 days prior the Treaty of Brussels) and 1 April 1948 that led to the "NATO" treaty being signed a year and three days later on the 4 April 1949.

And in good old German style, the German Defence Minister Ursula von der Leyen, welcomed the idea of a European Army. "Our future as

Europeans will at some point be with a European army," she told a German radio station.

As part of their "punishment", Germany, who couldn't be trusted to sustain an army following World War II, the Allies agreed to dissolve the Wehrmacht armed forces, that more or less ceased to exist by September 1945 and was officially dissolved by ACC Law 34 on 20 August 1946.

However, after the founding of the Federal Republic of Germany in May 1949 and because of its increasing links with the West under German chancellor Konrad Adenauer, the Consultative Assembly of Europe began to consider the formation of a European Defence Community with German participation on 11 August 1950.

Today, 2015 there's an approximate total of 60,500 soldiers on active service in the German Army.

DON'T MENTION ZEE VAR

Without sounding too pedantic and not wanting to insult anyone's intelligence or to teach those to suck eggs whose already fully knowledgeable on the subject of the world wars; as the subsequent brief information is for those who are not too familiar as to what took place in Europe during this period of time.

Particularly the younger voter who has been

deliberately indoctrinated to not pay too much heed or attention to the past "wars" or worry themselves too much about 'silly things' like 'voting' or 'politics' in general.

The following outlining material along with what else has been said on the topic within this book; is to perhaps help those understand the connection between that of the "founders" of the Treaty of Rome, their countries, the previous two world wars and possibly WWIII.

Why our leaders seem incapable to just keep themselves to themselves without the need to want to murder, rob and indoctrinate their "neighbours", yet naturally expect it from their own citizens whom 99.9% actually do comply is perhaps one of the biggest mysteries of them all.

It could be contended that if it wasn't for Germany, then the world may have not been at war, especially Europe; as it was Germany's Nazi regime and Adolf Hitler that started World War II, generally said to have begun on 1 September 1939 with the invasion of one of their neighbours Poland.

From late 1939 to early 1941, in a series of campaigns and treaties, Germany conquered or controlled much of continental Europe.

Following the Molotov–Ribbentrop Pact, Germany and the Soviet Union partitioned and annexed territories of their European neighbours, including

175

Poland, Finland and the Baltic states; Estonian, Latvian and Lithuanian.

However, what is equally intriguing is the build-up to WWI, and not the alleged cause of it;

'...the assassination of Archduke Franz Ferdinand and his wife Sophie on the 28 June 1914 by Gavrilo Princip, an ethnic Serb and Yugoslav nationalist from the group Young Bosnia,' - supported by the Black Hand nationalists in Serbia;

Yet it is the 'background' to this war and prior the assassinations that we need to pay heed to as they often say; - 'history has a habit of repeating itself.'

On November 29 1912, German Foreign Secretary Gottlieb von Jagow told the Reichstag (the German parliament), that; "If Austria is forced, for whatever reason, to fight for its position as a Great Power, then we must stand by her."

As a result, British Foreign Secretary Sir Edward Grey responded by warning Prince Karl Lichnowsky, the German Ambassador in London, that if Germany offered Austria a "blank cheque" for war in the Balkans, then "the consequences of such a policy would be incalculable."

To reinforce this point, R. B. Haldane, the Lord Chancellor, met with Prince Lichnowsky to offer an explicit warning, that if Germany were to attack France, Britain would intervene in France's favour.

And like with Russia's announcement of upping its defence spending by 30%+ in 2015, back then

176

Russian military reconstruction and the possibility of war was a leading topic at the German Imperial War Council of 8 December 1912 in Berlin, an informal meeting of some of Germany's top military leadership called on short notice by Kaiser Wilhelm II.

Attending the conference were the Kaiser, Admiral Alfred von Tirpitz – the Naval State Secretary, Admiral Georg Alexander von Müller, the Chief of the German Imperial Naval Cabinet (Marinekabinett), General Helmuth von Moltke – the Army's Chief of Staff, Admiral August von Heeringen – the Chief of the Naval General Staff and General Moriz von Lyncker, the Chief of the German Imperial Military Cabinet.

The presence of the leaders of both the German Army and Navy at this War Council attests to its importance. However, Chancellor Theobald von Bethmann-Hollweg and General Josias von Heeringen, the Prussian Minister of War, were not invited.

On the 11 February 2015 the four leaders of Russia, Germany, France and the Ukraine met for peace talks in Belarus on the Ukraine crisis and planning to sign a joint declaration supporting Ukraine's territorial integrity and sovereignty, a separate document was being prepared by the three-way 'contact group' comprising of Russia,

Ukraine and the Organisation for Security and Cooperation.

On the 5 March 2015, Ukraine's current president Petro Oleksiyovych, met the U.S. Secretary of State John Kerry, German Chancellor Anglea Merkel and French President Francois Hollande in Kiev to discuss the ongoing crisis in Ukraine.

On the 6 February 2015, Hollande and Merkel arrived in Moscow for talks on the Ukrainian crisis with President Vladimir Putin behind closed doors at the Kremlin – since these meetings a fragile ceasefire is in place.

At the 1912 meeting, Wilhelm II called British balance of power principles "idiocy," but agreed that Haldane's statement was a "desirable clarification" of British policy.

His opinion was that Austria should attack Serbia that December 1912, and if "Russia supports the Serbs, which she evidently does … then war would be unavoidable for us, too," and that would be better than going to war after Russia completed the massive modernisation and expansion of their army that they had just begun.

Moltke agreed that in his professional military opinion "a war is unavoidable and the sooner the better. Moltke "wanted to launch an immediate attack."

The rest is history, for as said before, world wars take some time to put into place; just over 18 months after the 8 December 2012 meeting, WWI began on 28 July 1914 and lasted until 11 November 1918. More than 9 million combatants and 7 million civilians died as a result of this unnecessary war.

The first world war had radically altered the political European map, with the defeat of the Central Powers—including Austria-Hungary, Germany and the Ottoman Empire—and the 1917 Bolshevik seizure of power in Russia.

Meanwhile, existing victorious Allies such as France, Belgium, Italy, Greece and Romania gained territories, and new Nation states were created out of the collapse of Austria-Hungary and the Ottoman and Russian Empires.

Despite the general public not having the stomach to fight such a war again, "recessions" alter everything that led to "Irredentism", the wanting to reclaim and reoccupy the lost regions as a direct result of WWI, termed the "homeland".

This leads to "Revanchism" ("revenge"), a term to describe a political manifestation of the will to reverse territorial losses incurred by a country, often following a war or social movement.

That ultimately turns into Nationalism that involves national identity, by contrast with the related construct of patriotism, which encompasses the social conditioning and personal behaviors that support a state's decisions and actions.

So it was with all these types of sentiments that especially cut their mark in Germany because of the significant territorial, colonial, and financial losses incurred by the Treaty of Versailles.

Under the treaty, Germany lost around 13 percent of its home territory and all of its overseas colonies, while German annexation of other states was prohibited, reparations were imposed, and limits were placed on the size and capability of the country's armed forces.

In addition, the Russian Civil War had led to the creation of the Soviet Union.

The German Empire was dissolved in the German Revolution of 1918–1919, and a democratic government, later known as the Weimar Republic, was created.

The interwar period saw strife between supporters of the new republic and hardline opponents on both the right and left.

Italy, being an Entente ally, with agreements with Britain and France had made some post-war territorial gains, however, Italian nationalists were angered that the promises made by Britain and France to secure Italian entrance into the war were not fulfilled with the peace settlement.

From 1922 to 1925, the Fascist movement led by Benito Mussolini seized power in Italy with a nationalist, totalitarian, and class collaborationist agenda that abolished representative democracy, repressed socialist, left-wing and liberal forces, and pursued an aggressive expansionist foreign policy aimed at forging Italy as a world power, promising the creation of a "New Roman Empire".

With the onset of the Great Depression in 1929, domestic support for Nazism and its leader Adolf Hitler rose and, in 1933, he was appointed Chancellor of Germany.

In the aftermath of the Reichstag fire, claimed by many to be a "false flag", Hitler could create a totalitarian single-party state led by the Nazis – opening the doors for Hitler to fulfil his lifelong plans.

Further afield, the Kuomintang (KMT) party in China launched a unification campaign against regional warlords and nominally unified China in the mid-1920s, but was soon embroiled in a civil war against its former Chinese communist allies.

In 1931, an increasingly militaristic Japanese Empire, which had long sought influence in China as the first step of what its government saw as the country's right to rule Asia, used the Mukden Incident as a pretext to launch the invasion of Manchuria and establish the puppet state of Manchukuo.

Too weak to resist Japan, China appealed to the League of Nations for help.

Japan withdrew from the League of Nations after being condemned for its incursion into Manchuria.

The two nations then fought several battles, in Shanghai, Rehe and Hebei, until the Tanggu Truce was signed in 1933. Thereafter, Chinese volunteer forces continued the resistance to Japanese aggression in Manchuria, and Chahar and Suiyuan.

Adolf Hitler, after an unsuccessful attempt to overthrow the German government in 1923, eventually became the Chancellor of Germany in 1933.

He abolished democracy, espousing a radical, racially motivated revision of the world order, and soon began a massive rearmament campaign.

It was at this time that multiple political scientists began to predict that a second Great War might take place.

Meanwhile, France, to secure its alliance, allowed Italy a free hand in Ethiopia, which Italy desired as a colonial possession.

The situation was aggravated in early 1935 when the Territory of the Saar Basin was legally reunited with Germany and Hitler repudiated the Treaty of Versailles, accelerated his rearmament programme and introduced conscription.

Hoping to contain Germany, the United Kingdom, France and Italy formed the Stresa Front; however, in June 1935, the United Kingdom made an independent naval agreement with Germany, easing prior restrictions.

The Soviet Union, concerned due to Germany's goals of capturing vast areas of Eastern Europe, wrote a treaty of mutual assistance with France. Before taking effect though, the Franco-Soviet pact was required to go through the bureaucracy of the League of Nations, which rendered it essentially toothless.

It's then alleged that the United States, being concerned with events in Europe and Asia, passed the Neutrality Act in August of the same year.

Two months later, Italy invaded Ethiopia through Italian Somaliland and Eritrea; Germany was the only major European nation to support the invasion.

Italy subsequently dropped its objections to Germany's goal of absorbing Austria.

Hitler defied the Versailles and Locarno treaties by remilitarising the Rhineland in March 1936.

He received little response from other European powers; for like said, wars are as much in the interest of the 1% as is big business in peacetime.

When the Spanish Civil War broke out in July, Hitler and Mussolini supported the fascist and authoritarian Nationalist forces in their civil war against the Soviet-supported Spanish Republic.

Both sides used the conflict to test new weapons and methods of warfare, with the Nationalists winning the war in early 1939.

In October 1936, Germany and Italy formed the Rome–Berlin Axis. A month later, Germany and

Japan signed the Anti-Comintern Pact, which Italy would join in the following year.

In China, after the Xi'an Incident, the Kuomintang and communist forces agreed on a ceasefire to present a united front to oppose Japan.

Germany, Italy and Japan were known as the Axis of nations that fought in WWII against the Allied forces. The Axis powers were united by their opposition to several Western powers and the Soviet Union.

Germany's allies were; Austria (as part of Germany), Bulgaria, Croatia, Finland, Hungary, Iraq, Romania, Slovakia, Thailand and Japan with a number of puppet states and regimes that provided assistance; Albania, Vichy France, Portugal and even Burma.

Spain did not participate in war, but was supporting the Axis. The same could be said about Denmark, as officially they remained neutral, yet history reveals elsewise and was occupied by Germany throughout the war.

Afghanistan, Portugal, Sweden and Switzerland remained neutral throughout the war. While the Northern Irish fought on the Allied side, the remainder of the Republic of Eire stayed neutral.

Some countries in the Americas remained neutral until the closing few months of the war. These included Andorra, Argentina, Chile, Guatemala, Liechtenstein, Saudi Arabia and Yemen.

The Allies of World War II, called the United Nations from the 1 January 1942 declaration, were the countries that opposed the above quoted Axis of nations.

The major affiliated state combatants were; Britain, China, Soviet Union, United States and France - that see itself spilt and with the Vichy of France supporting Germany. The minor affiliated state combatants were; Australia, Belgium, Brazil, Canada, Czechoslovakia, Greece, Luxembourg, Mexico, Netherlands, New Zealand, Norway, Poland, South Africa, Yugoslavia. Like France, Albania was divided with their support.

After World War II, moves towards European integration were seen by many as an escape from the extreme forms of nationalism that had devastated the continent.

1952 saw the creation of the European Coal and Steel Community, (ECSC) which was declared to be "a first step in the federation of Europe", starting with the aim of eliminating the possibility of further wars between its member states by means of pooling their national heavy industries.

The founding members of the Community, known

as the "inner six", were Belgium, France, Italy, Luxembourg, the Netherlands, and West Germany, that was of course Germany during and prior the war.

That means the "Common Market" Treaty of Rome was ratified and established by the two main powers of the Axis, Germany and Italy, along with two minor affiliated state combatants of the Allies - Belgium and the Netherlands (Luxembourg) and France whom at one time the Vichy of France and its appointed Premier of France by President Albert Lebrun, Marshal Pétain had ordered his men to sign the armistice with Germany on 22 June 1940.

Arguably these former countries are hardly the safest of foundations on which to build a European interest group on.

A group that would now wish to benefit it's not so long ago enemies who had annihilated and razed their countries to the ground.

Perhaps this kind of retroact is ultimate proof it's the 1% who are behind all wars and why they can simply brush the dust off their clothing and start all over again as if nothing really took place in the first place.

A group who essentially are masterminded by the very same men who sustained a regime who passionately believed in an ideology of a supreme Aryan master-race, that even countries regions such as the Vichy of France, whose own authorities were brought in to round up Jews and other "undesirables" deemed as "communists" or political refugees - were drawn into this murderous belief-system, as was Italy with their obsession of a Roman Empire.

Much of the French public initially supported the new government despite its undemocratic and pro-Axis policies, often seeing it as necessary to maintain a degree of French autonomy and territorial integrity.

They established their own authoritarian regime by gaining full powers on 10 July 1940 to replace the French Third Republic that was dissolved.

Calling for "National Regeneration," Vichy reversed many liberal policies and began tight supervision of the economy with central planning and austerity measures a key feature.

"Labour" unions came under tight government control. There were no elections. The independence of women was reversed, with an emphasis put on motherhood, as they knew millions of innocent men, women and children would be exterminated and need fresh human cannon fodder.

And again the rest is history; it was the most widespread war in history, and directly involved more than 100 million people from over 30 countries.

In a state of "total war", the major participants threw their entire economic, industrial, and scientific capabilities behind the war effort, erasing the distinction between civilian and military resources.

Marked by mass deaths of civilians, including the Holocaust and the strategic bombing of industrial and population centres (during which approximately one million people were killed, including the use of two nuclear weapons in combat), it resulted in an estimated 50 million to 85 million fatalities.

This made World War II the deadliest conflict in human history from 1st September 1939 to 2nd September 1945.

Sadly, it looks inevitable that WWII is on the cards and despite believing we learn from our mistakes, history sure does have a habitual problem of relapsing and ignoring all the rehabilitation it took to recover from such an addiction to war, and doing it all over again.

Yet oddly enough it's not the seven billion or so residents on the planet who are the junkies, but that 1% who can't or simply don't want to remain clean and kick their bad habits.

Who knows what the answer really is or what is the right thing to do?

Perhaps, if a new elected British government, that again oddly could be UKIP as they are the only ones brave and bold enough to tear-up those 'treaties' that previous governments had assigned their unwilling and ignorant to the facts and implications nation up to - and that were the UK to withdraw from the EU; and that were there ever to be another outbreak of war in Europe;

that with its secure borders back in place it goes without saying the country would probably be far better off following a neutral stance and as the previously above quoted countries did, such as Southern Ireland.

For were the British general public truly aware of the reality and specifics that surrounds the Treaty of Rome that in turn led on to a series of other treaties being drafted and formed, including the Maastricht and Lisbon Treaties, then it's pretty certain the vast majority wouldn't have endorsed them in anyway whatsoever, and "they" probably chose to ignore them in the first place.

THE NAZI ROOTS OF BRUSSELS

Then with knowing of Germany's track-record with two world wars under its belt, you'd think the last person to reside over the presidency of European Commission would be an ex-member of Hitler's Nazi regime.

The Hallstein Commission is the European Commission that held office from 7 January 1958 to

30 June 1967. Its president and key architect, was Walter Hallstein and held two separate mandates.

We haven't the time or space, nor is it our intention to cover every aspect of the European Commission and if you'd like to know more of this rather alarming story then perhaps you'd like to read the following books titled;

"The Nazi Roots of the Brussels EU" by Paul Anthony Taylor, Aleksandra Niedzwiecki, Matthias Rath and August Kowalczyk, published by Dr. Rath Health Foundation 2010;

Arno Sölters' book; The Greater Sphere Cartel.

In order to help give you some idea as to who was really behind the formation of the "Common Market", in this and the following chapter we've included some extracts from these quoted books.

Like many untrue things on the internet and written about on various subjects; there are also 'false' biographies, especially on pages such as Wikipedia and where those behind the writing and uploading of the details, have their own hidden agendas.

Often they wish to paint a different picture, as to otherwise let the truth be known would seriously undermine what it is they are trying to endorse. So they will skirt around certain issues though not come-up with any definite or precise details, and this is often the case about any ex-member of Hitler's

Nazi regime, including Walter Hallstien.

Hallstien is often painted as a whiter-than-white member of the Nazi's, and didn't really have too much to do with all the horrifying and repulsive stuff the Germans got up to.

However, there are many historians and authors, such as those just mentioned above who have since been able to gain records and archive material to be able to prove, that Walter Hallstien had much more involvement in the Nazi regime than what many had previously been led to believe.

Hallstein was a member of both the National Socialist Association of German Legal Professionals, an organisation of German legal professionals (lawyers, judges, public prosecutors, notaries and legal academics) in the Third Reich from 1936 to 1945, and the infamous 'Nazi Rechts-wahrer' Organisation.

Membership in this organisation was restricted to those individuals showing unconditional and uncompromising support for, and the participation in the implementation of the Nazi ideology and regime planning for the conquest of the world by the Nazi government/IG Farben coalition.

IG Farben was a German chemical industry conglomerate, notorious for its role in the Holocaust. Its name is taken from Interessen-Gemeinschaft Farbenindustrie AG (Syndicate [literally, "community of interests"] of dye-making corporations).

The company was formed in 1925 from a number of major chemical companies that had been working together closely since World War I. During its heyday, IG Farben was the largest chemical company in the world and the fourth largest overall industrial concern, after General Motors, U.S. Steel, and Standard Oil of New Jersey.

Following the Nazi takeover of Germany, IG Farben became involved in numerous war crimes during World War II.

Most notoriously, the firm's pro-Nazi leadership openly and knowingly collaborated with the Nazi government to produce the large quantities of Zyklon B necessary to gas to death millions of Jews and other "undesirables", including some who so happened to believe in communism, at various extermination camps during the Holocaust.

The firm ceased operating following the fall of Nazi Germany in 1945, when the company was seized by the Allies; its assets were entirely liquidated in 1952, and 13 executives were imprisoned for terms ranging from 1 to 8 years at the Nuremberg Trials (specifically, the IG Farben Trial) for their roles in the atrocities.

Engulfed by lawsuits and universal condemnation after the war's end, the company continued to exist as a shell with the sole stated goal of continuing to do business so it may pay many millions of marks in reparations to the victims of its many crimes. It has been criticised over the years for paying almost nothing in claims.

THE GREATER SPHERE CARTEL

The following is an extract from; "The Nazi Roots of the Brussels EU", Chapter 3. The comments in (brackets) were made by the authors of this same book;
Walter Hallstein was by no means the only architect of a post-WWII world under the control of the Nazi/Cartel Coalition.

By 1941, the Nazi regime was maintaining several official 'institutes' with one purpose only: Preparing the future economic and political shape of the world – to be established after a Nazi/Cartel victory in WWII.

One of these 'conquest institutes' was the "Central Research Institute for National Economic Order and Greater Sphere Economy" in Dresden, Germany.'

In 1941, Arno Söelter summarised the Nazi/Cartel plans for a post-WWII Europe under their control in his book: "The Greater Sphere Cartel – An Instrument of Industrial Market Order in a New Europe." [The original German title was: "Das Großraum-Kartell-Ein Instrument der industriellen Marktordnung in einem neuen Europa"].

194

The German word Großraum, or "großer Raum," literally means greater space or greater sphere.

Söelters' book became a blueprint for the 'Brussels EU'. The parallels are breath-taking. The publication of his was not the act of an individual. Sölter was head of the official Nazi "Central Research Institute for National Economic Order and Greater Sphere Economy" in Dresden, Germany, at that time.

This "Institute" was one of the official economic planning offices of the Nazi/Farben coalition for post-war Europe.

This book provides the blueprint of what would later become the structure of the European Union – a body of cartel interests, claiming "greater spheres" as their markets – and operating beyond any democratic control.

The following detailed description of the I.G. Farben post-WWII plans were published in The Greater Sphere Cartel;

By summer 1941 the coalition of the oil and drug (pharmaceutical) cartel I.G. Farben – Bayer, BASF, Hoechst (today a part of Sanofi-Aventis) – and their political/military stakeholders, the Nazis, had occupied France and brutally conquered large parts of Europe.

It was at this time that the oil and drug cartel I.G. Farben started to reveal its post-war plans. After financing the rise of the Nazis and the build-up of their war machinery (providing almost 100% of explosives, gasoline, rubber and most other war essentials) the oil and drug cartel was looking for an exorbitant "return on investment."

These facts are detailed in the 1945 US Congressional hearings about I.G. Farben and in the Nuremberg War Crimes Tribunals against this cartel.

The I.G. Farben cartel got its "return on investment." From the roughly 20 countries brutally conquered by the Nazi troops. I.G. Farben received essentially all of the chemical, pharmaceutical, petrochemical, mineral and other industries – mostly for free.

Behind every tank that rolled into Belgium, the Netherlands, France, Poland, Czechoslovakia, Denmark, Norway and all the other European countries, followed the "men in grey," the corporate representatives of I.G. Farben to seize their booty.

(This unscrupulous plunder of entire industries and countries became the blueprint for subsequent global heists – up to the present day: Haliburton, various oil and drug multinationals as well other corporate "investors" in the Bush presidency made sure they got their "return on investment" during the Iraq war.)

The I.G. Farben terminology of a post-war rule over a "greater sphere" initially described the territory of Europe including Russia. But this term was deliberately kept flexible so that - with the projected military victories over Asia, America and the rest of the world – the term "greater sphere" would comprise the entire globe.

These plans for military world conquest and subsequent economic subjugation by the Nazi/I.G. Farben coalition are detailed in the Nuremberg War Crimes Tribunals against the directors of the I.G. Farben concern.

Copies of more than 40,000 original documents of this historic trial from the U.S. National Archives were hidden away from the public for 6 decades.

The following is also an extract from "The Greater Sphere Cartel"; the text in [parentheses] are added commentaries from the authors of "The Nazi Roots of the Brussels EU", who too included the following extract in their book;

We recall the market organisation hierarchy: State – Economic Group – Cartel, which we have established for the Greater Sphere. In this connection, we are disregarding the state's responsibilities in the field of commercial and currency policy within the Greater Sphere.

Instead we want to look in greater detail at the problem of the organisation of the European market from a cartel point of view and subsequently, look in detail at the problems of the economic policies of the state, which inevitably result due to the principle market regulation of the whole area of the 'Großraum-Kartell'.

Directly in charge of the "Großraum-Kartell" is the Economic Group, whose market-regulating functions, we want to see brought together in a 'Cartel Office.'

To this end the existing cartel department for the Economic Groups would have to be expanded to take on the functions of this new office.

Superior to the Cartel Office would be the Central Cartel Office, which on grounds of the remit assigned to it would correspond to the present 'Cartel Supervision' department of the German Industry Group (Reichsgruppe Industrie), but also to the cartel department or specialist departments of the German Ministry for Economic Affairs.

(Note: Today's EU-Commission is an exact copy of this "Central Cartel Office." It rules on behalf of cartel interests and beyond any democratic control.)

From a practical point of view the tasks would have to be divided in order to avoid the duplication of work.

It would be expedient to assign the factual supervision of the cartel offices to the Ministry for Economic Affairs, whereas the duties of the Central Cartel Office for Industry would be more in dealing with questions of fundamental market organisation, as well as legal and interstate cartel questions.

In order to operate effectively, the Office for

Industry would have to be kept informed about any problems arising. If we subsequently discuss the objectives of the "Central Cartel Office" we shall also discuss the associated business and organisational problems, i.e. those not itemised according to the above mentioned authorities.

It naturally follows that the German method of cartel supervision will also be introduced in the non-German parts of the European Sphere of Influence.

The extent and nature of the organisation in other countries would naturally vary depending on their degree of industrialisation.

Below we discuss the mode of operation of the organisation of the cartel in relation to the prevailing conditions in Germany;

a) The Central Cartel Office is the highest regulatory authority, accordingly it is;

i) Responsible for taking final decisions on questions of areas of responsibility of the cartel supervision;

ii) Responsible for maintaining close contact with the highest expert bodies (i.e. economic and trading policies, pricing policies, commodity policies, etc.) and for coordinating with said expert bodies its subject-related decisions and fundamental instructions to subordinate institutions.

b) The Central Cartel Office maintains contact with possible central national cartel offices of the other European countries both in terms of dealing with important fundamental issues and concerning decisions about areas of responsibility that the 'Großraum-Kartell' or the individual national cartels cannot agree upon.

c) Accordingly, the Central Cartel Office represents the appropriate complaint department about the decisions taken by cartel offices. Furthermore, complaints concerning such matters as action taken and infringements committed by foreign cartels should be made via the Central Cartel Office.

d) Cartel law, which is currently very diverse and poorly organized would have to be reformed and as far as possible standardised for entire greater sphere.

[Note: More than 6 decades later the EU-Commission implements an almost exact copy of this plan with the goal to establish "standardized cartel law" to rule over the lives of almost 500 million Europeans – without any democratic control.]

e) General market regulation principles for the European Greater Sphere would have to be drawn up. As regards to market- and cartel regulation, similar rules have to be established, just like those economic decrees that have been worked out or rather, are still worked on, by the Ministry for Economic Affairs for the accounting system.

(Note: A few decades later, the Nazi/I.G. Farben "Cartel decrees" became "EU-Directives" ruling not only over the health and lives of the peoples of Europe but also draining their economies.)

f) In business economics, too, cooperation with non-German countries must be introduced in order to be able to prepare sound market regulation (including intercompany comparisons).

g) A model organisational plan for a "Großraum-Kartell" would have to be drawn up, along with clear, simple model of articles of association. To ensure effective cartel supervision a suitably-drafted cartel agreement is indispensible. Due to historical developments and often countless changes in contractual provisions, many cartel agreements end up becoming completely impenetrable. Therefore, in future, a suitably-formulated master agreement must be finalised which governs the details of any ongoing changes or supplementary agreements.

(Note: This "master agreement" became the EU's so called "Lisbon Treaty" – an "enabling law" that grants quasi-dictatorial powers to the cartels "EU Commission". For good reason, the cartel is not allowing a democratic referendum on this "master agreement" for fear of rejection. The people of the only country that voted on it, Ireland, sent a resounding "No" to the "central cartel office" – the EU Commission in Brussels.)

h) Suitable unified classification schemes must also be devised for cartel production and distribution statistics. The sales statistics must be laid out in such a way that at any time distribution can be adjusted according to consumption needs.

i) A central cartel register must be set up including not just German but also international participants in all areas of influence of the "Großraum-Kartell". The cartel register must include both the nature of agreements reached and details of commodity procurement, business premises, production conditions and the like. To a degree the register must represent a mirror image of the "Großraum-Kartell" as a whole.

j) The Central Cartel Office would have to arrange the publication of a journal entitled "Das Großraum-Kartell" ("The Greater Sphere Cartel"), which would publish all decisions of the highest authority on all fundamental questions of European market regulation, directives and similar matters.

(Note: This point too was adapted by the Brussels EU. They issue the "Official Journal of the European Union, as their "legal gazette." No regulation or directive can become law until it has been published in this gazette.)

THE TREATIES

The European Coal and Steel Community (ECSC), forerunner of the European Economic Community (EEC), was established under the Treaty of Paris

(1951). The negotiations that led to the Treaty of Rome began at Messina, Italy in 1955. The Treaty was signed in Rome in March 1957 and came into force in January 1958.

The 1992 Maastricht Treaty (formally, the Treaty on European Union or TEU), superseded the Treaty of Rome, - undertaken to integrate Europe it was signed on the 7 February 1992 by the members of the European Community in Maastricht, Netherlands.

On 9–10 December 1991, the same city hosted the European Council which drafted the treaty. Upon its entry into force on 1 November 1993 during the Delors Commission, it created the European Union and led to the creation of the single European currency, the euro.

The Maastricht Treaty has been amended by the treaties of Amsterdam, Nice and Lisbon.

The treaty led to the creation of the euro. One of the obligations of the treaty for the members was to keep "sound fiscal policies, with debt limited to 60% of GDP and annual deficits no greater than 3% of GDP."

And it's this obligation following the worlds recession that many member states have been unable to successful fulfil.

The treaty also established the three pillars of the European Union, one supranational pillar created from three European Communities which includes;

- European Coal and Steel Community (ECSC).
- The Eurasian Economic Community (EAEC or EurAsEC) and EC (European Community), - and the Common Foreign and Security Policy (CFSP) pillar.
- The Justice and Home Affairs (JHA) pillar.

Coordination in foreign policy had taken place since the beginning of the 1970s under the name of European Political Cooperation (EPC), which had been first written into the treaties by the Single European Act but not as a part of the EEC.

While the Justice and Home Affairs pillar extended cooperation in law enforcement, criminal justice, asylum, and immigration and judicial cooperation in civil matters.

The Treaty of Lisbon (initially known as the Reform Treaty) is an international agreement which amends the two treaties which form the constitutional basis of the European Union (EU).

The Treaty of Lisbon was signed by the EU member states on 13 December 2007, and entered into force on 1 December 2009.

It amends the Maastricht Treaty (1993), which also is known as the Treaty on European Union, and the Treaty of Rome (1958), which also is known as the Treaty establishing the European Community (TEEC).

At Lisbon, the Treaty of Rome was renamed to the Treaty on the Functioning of the European Union (TFEU).

Prominent changes included the move from unanimity to qualified majority voting in at least 45 policy areas in the Council of Ministers, a change in calculating such a majority to a new double majority, a more powerful European Parliament forming a bicameral legislature alongside the Council of Ministers under the ordinary legislative procedure, a consolidated legal personality for the EU and the creation of a long-term President of the European Council and a High Representative of the Union for Foreign Affairs and Security Policy.

It was originally intended to have been ratified by all member states by the end of 2008. This timetable failed, primarily due to the initial rejection of the Treaty in 2008 by the Irish electorate, a decision which was reversed in a second referendum in 2009 after Ireland secured a number of concessions related to the treaty.

Joining the Common Market or What the Treaty of Rome Means, was a small (12cm x 18cm) 13 page* booklet that sold for sixpence, and first published in 1967 by Political Intelligence Publications Ltd.

The "original" booklet, is as rare as hen's teeth with probably the vast majority of printed copies since being disposed of.

Existing copies may lay hidden away or forgotten about in the bottom of a desk, draw-or cupboard, - or proudly on display at the HQ of political parties and interest groups, such as the Get Britain Out campaign, the Campaign for an Independent Britain or the UK Independence Party;

as interestingly enough it discloses the same type of retroact, stance and argument, though not to exit the European Union, - but for the country to never enter it.

If there are any copies of this booklet laying around, then it's possibly a copy of a 1970, 14 page version.

The title is the same, yet its contents are slightly different; published three years later by the Anti-Common Market League (ACML), which too is virtually impossible to source other than there is a copy in the archives of the London School of Economics.

The European Union Institutions archive holds a paper reference to the 1967 booklet, but not its contents.

Even though they were 'one-off editions', they read somewhat like an almanac, as the transcript attempts to forecast, inform and pre-warn the reader of a list of detrimental set of events that are forthcoming to the shores of the United Kingdom, if "she" was to ever join the 'Common Market' and why its contents are as contemporary today than it ever was 48 years ago.

The following is the contents of the original 1967 - Joining the Common Market – What the Treaty of Rome Means. All text is verbatim other than when – seen (in brackets), these additional words were recently added by us.

EXPLANATION

If Britain wants to join the European Common Market, there is only one way of doing so: she must sign the Treaty of Rome and belong to the European Economic Community.

Very few people have yet read, or are ever likely to have time to read, the full Treaty of 248 Articles, 4 Annexes and 15 protocols and conventions. As Sir Harry Legge-Bourke, M.P., said in Parliament (16th

November, 1966), "...probably very few hon. Members, and certainly the vast majority of people in the country have never read this document. I am afraid that many Ministers and ex-Ministers have never read it."

So, this booklet explains the Treaty of Rome in simple terms and quotes some important parts of it.

INTRODUCTION

The Common Market consists of Belgium, France, Germany, Holland, Italy and Luxemburg. They signed the Treaty of Rome on the 25th March 1957, to start the European Economic Community (EEC) on the 1st January 1958.

EEC is not just a matter of trade and tariffs as many people like to think. It covers a vast range of social and economic matters-in fact, only defence and foreign policy are, for the time being, really outside it.

In the words of its Commission's President (Walter Hallstein): "We are not in business to promote tariff preferences, to establish a discriminatory club, to form a larger market to make us richer, or a trading bloc to further our commercial interests. We are not in business at all: we are in politics."

When the British parliament in August 1961 first approved of negotiations, few M.P.s were even in possession of an authorised English version of the Treaty, which had only been available to them for less than a month. Yet, signing the Treaty of Rome has the following consequences, among many others:-

1.   No nation can ever, legitimately, of its own sole free will, withdraw (see page 12);

2.   All members accept a superior form of government, in shape of the EEC institutions (see page 6);

3.   Every member must accept majority decisions on policy, even if policy harms them (see page 7);

4.   A Commission of nine civil servants in Brussels has far-reaching powers to issue regulations, binding on all countries whatever their national parliaments may wish (see page 7);

5.   The say which every ordinary individual has to-day, through his vote, in the running of his country grows less and less, because elected parliaments dwindle in importance and the unelected European officials become more powerful.

These and other matters are covered and explained in the following pages, with extracts from the Treaty itself.

People in Britain sometimes cherish the hope that alterations can comfortably be made to the Treaty, to accommodate British reservations and allow them the best of both worlds. This is as dangerous illusion, which few knowledgeable people share.

If Britain were to ever join the EEC, she would have to accept the Treaty as it stands-its "disciplines", as the French describe it, "without reservations." So, too, would other aspiring new members.

The Conservative Party's leader, Edward Heath, has said (Hansard-17th November 1966) "...we should frankly recognise this surrender of sovereignty and its purpose...We accept the Treaty of Rome unequivocally."

(1) THE TREATY PROVISIONS

THE AIMS AND OBJECTS are set out in ARTICLE 3 as follows:-

(a) the elimination, as between Member States, of customs duties and of quantitative restrictions on the import and export of goods, and of all other measures having equivalent effect;

(b) the establishment of a common customs tariff and of a common commercial policy towards third countries;

(c) the abolition, as between Member States, of obstacles to freedom of movement for persons, services and capital;

(d) the adoption of a common policy in the sphere of agriculture;

(e) the adoption of a common policy in the sphere of transport;

(f) the institution of a system ensuring that competition in the common market is not distorted;

(g) the application of procedures by which the economic policies of Member States can he co-ordinated and disequilibria in their balances of payments remedied;

(h) the approximation of the laws of Member States to the extent required for the proper functioning of the common market;

(i) the creation of a European Social Fund in order to improve employment opportunities for workers and to contribute to the raising of their standard of living;

(j) the establishment of a European Investment Bank to facilitate the economic expansion of the Community by opening up fresh resources;

(k) the association of the overseas countries and territories in order to increase trade and to promote jointly economic and social development.

Of these eleven activities, it will be seen that only two refer to tariffs and customs duties, or Common Market. The remaining nine cover the widest of political issues; this is not understood in Britain where politicians have preferred to avoid explaining the extent of the political implications.

(2) THE INSTITUTIONS

Ruling EEC are set out in ARTICLE 4:

an ASSEMBLY
a COUNCIL,
a COMMISSION,
a COURT OF JUSTICE.

These Community institutions were accepted unreservedly by the British government in 1961, and the present government has made no reservations about them since.

Yet, together they constitute a form of supra-national government, superior to Britain's parliament and at variance with many of the inherent liberties and traditions of British life.

The formal nature of these institutions themselves reflects the Continental attachment to rigid paper constitutions, and contrasts with Britain's more flexible approach to constitutional problems.

The British system has nonetheless lasted and developed over 700 years evolving parliamentary government; the main members of the Common Market have all themselves had brand new constitutions within the last 21 years, following many revisions this century alone.

(a) THE ASSEMBLY

The least effective of the EEC institutions is the Assembly, sometimes named the European Parliament. Elaborated in Articles 137 to 144, it consists of nominated – not elected – delegates in set proportions from the six member states, meeting in annual session each October.

It has no legislative powers, and is only real sanction lies in Article 144, which provides for the Assembly dismissing the whole of the Community's Commission, if a vote of censure is carried by two-thirds majority of members voting.

(b) THE COUNCIL

Of much greater importance in the institutional set-up is the Council, which is given specific powers by Articles 145 to 154. The Council consists of one member from each state and, broadly, takes the decision on the policies to be followed in the Community.

In doing so, it reaches all but a few reserved decisions either by a majority of its members or in specific cases by a qualified majority, in which France, Germany and Italy have 4 votes each, Belgium and Holland 2 each and Luxembourg 1. In the total voting strength of 17, a qualified majority consists of 12 votes in favour, from four members.

The Treaty's provisions thus effectively preclude any one member from dominating the others, but a majority of four members with enough votes is sufficient for the adoptions of policies which could be harmful to the remaining one or two.

If Britain joined, she would probably have 4 votes out a total of 21. If other countries joined, the total could rise to 30 or 35. Thus Britain would never have a better say in the management of her own affairs than 4/21ths.

This reality must always be faced: if Britain, with her substantially different interests all over the world, joined the EEC she could by majority of voting be forced into adopting of policies hostile to her true interests.   This is the case right from the very beginning over farming and food.

(c) THE COMMISSION

The Commission consists of nine officials drawn from the six member states, who are forbidden to seek or take instructions from any government or other body. Covered by Articles 155 to 163, their role is defined in Article 155, to;

"ensure that the provisions of this Treaty and the measures taken by the institutions pursuant thereto are applied;

"formulate recommendations or deliver opinions on matters dealt with in this Treaty, if it expressly so provides or if the Commission considers it necessary;

"have its own power of decision and participate in the shaping of measures taken by the Council and by the Assembly [European Parliament] in the manner provided for in this Treaty;

"exercise the powers conferred on it by the Council for the implementation of the rules laid down by the latter."

(d) THE COURT OF JUSTICE

This is covered by 25 Articles (164 to 188). It is a type of court foreign to the British legal system. The greatest difference has always existed between the Continental system of jurisprudence, founded upon Byzantine Roman Law, and the customary Common Law of England.

The contrast is most marked in the sphere on criminal procedure, and nowhere more so than between the English tradition that a man is held innocent until the prosecution proves otherwise and the continental requirement for the accused to prove his innocence.

Highly significant, too, is the difference between the safeguards here of habeas corpus and appearance in court within a day of arrest, and the long periods which an accused person can languish untried in jails in France, Germany, Holland and Italy.

Criminal procedure might well not be affected by British membership of EEC for some time, but in the realms of constitutional and civil law the effect would be immediate. (See below. Item 4).

The Treaty of Rome is a Continental treaty based on Continental concepts differing greatly from British concepts of law, order and good government- but it is the British concepts which would have to go.

Parliament would be compelled to undertake the most comprehensive revision of all British law, to bring it into line; everything conflicting with the Rome Treaty would have to be repealed or amended, even if every single MP (elected by the British people) wanted it to remain as it was.

(4) POWER

The great powers of the EEC are set out in Articles 189 to 192. The most important is 189, which says;

"The Council and the Commission shall, in the discharge of their duties and in accordance with the provisions of this Treaty, issue regulations and directives, take decisions and formulate recommendations or opinions.

Regulations shall have general application. They shall be binding in every respect and directly applicable in each Member State.

Directives shall be binding, in respect of the result to be achieved, upon every Member State, but the form and manner of enforcing them shall be a matter for the national authorities.

Decisions shall be binding in every respect upon

those to whom they are directed.

Recommendations and opinions shall have no binding force."

The powers invested in the Commission are superior to national parliaments, which can only be reduced to the role of rubber stamps. They are powerless to amend EEC regulations, even if they violate many principles of British justice.

As Roy Price, formerly Common Market press officer in London, explained in his book "The Political Future of the European Community":-

"In any case a national parliament has no direct say in the preliminary-and decisive-work of the Commission, nor in the subsequent stages by which the Commission's proposal becomes law. As more and more decisions are taken by majority vote even the semblance of influence disappears, for even if the national government concerned maintains its opposition to the bitter end it can still be out-voted, and the minister concerned can only then report the fact of the decision to his national assembly."

A good warning for British businessmen is in regulation 17, issued in accordance with Articles 85 and 86 of the Treaty, which deal with competition between members of the Common Market. The regulations takes power for the Commission's servants to examine books and other business documents, to makes copies or extracts, to demand oral explanations on the spot, and to have access to all premises, land and vehicles.

Later, the same regulations takes the power to inflict huge monetary penalties on businesses, according to the decisions of the Commission. The regulation is noteworthy because the Commission combines the roles of executives, judge and jury; no impartially-granted search warrant has to be sought for the first lot of powers, and no impartially-adjudicated hearing is provided before the levying of penalties.

(5) AGRICULTURE

The Common Market's policy for agriculture comes under Articles 38 to 47, to include fish, animal fats and margarine, wine and fermented beverages, tobacco, cork, flax and hemp.

Britain would be required to adopt the EEC policy of higher home prices (and no subsidies to farmers), with first place for imports going to dearer European produce in place of economically priced food from Australia, New Zealand and Canada. Any imports from these latter countries would be made deliberately dearer by imports levies, payable to EEC funds.

(6) FREE MOVEMENT OF LABOUR

There is to be a Common Market in people, as well as in capitals and services. Twenty-six Articles (48 to 73) elaborate the policy for the free movement of labour, the right of establishment, and the abolition of restrictions on monetary transfers.

Workers are specifically to have the right to move freely between the territories of all member states, and to stay in another member state for employment, and to remain there or change jobs without restriction.

A system is to be introduced for paying social security benefits to persons where they are resident, and for all qualifying periods for benefits under the domestic legislation of the countries concerned to be added together. Any discrimination on the ground of nationality is prohibited.

It follows that the powers granted by Parliament under the Commonwealth Immigrants Act to control immigration from the Commonwealth could not be applied at all to European immigration if Britain joins the Common Market.

(7) COMMON TRANSPORT POLICY

A common policy for transport is the subject of Articles 74 to 84, to cover rail, road and inland waterways. By unanimous decision sea and air transport could be included. Common rules applicable to international transport, and for non-resident transport concerns operating in a member state are to be laid down, and within the Community all discrimination because of country of origin or destination is to be removed.

Also prohibited are any changes and conditions by a member state, which involve any element of support or protection for a particular undertaking or industry.

(8) THE APPROXIMATION OF NATIONAL LAWS

This is set out in Articles 100 to 102. The Council can-by unanimous decision-issue directives to member states on this, requiring the approximation of such legislative and administration provisions as directly affect the establishment or operation of the Common Market.

This is very wide provision, which could Ultimately be interpreted and made to cover much more ground than may at present be intended.

("Therefore it is obviously not acceptable that the Legal System – that represents the blood circulation of this Body is being strangulated by the diversity of legal systems in its different parts..." - Hallstein's 1939 'Conquest Speech.' - The 'diversity of legal systems' – such as the UK's 'Trial by jury', Magna Carta and Democratic voting system; all fundamental 'rights of man' are viewed upon by Hallstien as an impediment to the unelected self-appointed 'we know better than you' commission of bureaucrats that head the EU.)

(9) THE BALANCE OF PAYMENTS

A member's right to take action to safeguard any balance of payments problem is limited by the six Articles 104 to 109. They require collaboration between member states, to coordinate their economic policies for the purpose of achieving the right one to ensure overall equilibrium in their balance of payments.

The Commission has the right to investigate the financial situation of any member state which is in difficulties and liable to affect the Common Market, and to suggest measures for improving the position.

Mutual assistance may be offered by the Council, and only if this is not done may the member state in difficulties be allowed to take protective measures authorised by the Commission.

Clearly, the problems of the sterling area would be soon become the direct business of the Commission, and Britain's freedom to deal with them would be severely circumscribed, were this country in the EEC.

(Let's not forget George Osborne's outrageous untrue claim, that he halved the UK's European bill, as the UK stilled owed the full £1.7 billion, though half was paid in December 2014. The remainder was simply offset with its usual rebate on EU contributions, thus he didn't actually save the country a single pound.)

(10) TRADE WITH OTHER COUNTRIES

This is dealt with in seven Articles (110 to 116), which embody one of the biggest surrenders of national sovereignty, Article 113 places with the Commission the conduct of negotiations for trade agreements with third countries. Approval rests with the Council, which may act by qualified majority vote.

For Britain, this would mean that membership of EEC precluded this country from negotiating direct agreements on trade with countries such as Australia and New Zealand. Any desired arrangement would have to be subject to a majority agreement by the Council, with negotiations being carried out by noting that in 1965, less than 20 per cent of Britain's exports went to the Common Market, and over 80 per cent to rest of the world. So, four-fifths of Britain trade could be jeopardised by inability to make better arrangements with third countries, because of Article 113.

(11) FREE TRADE AND DISCRIMINATION

A total of 29 Articles (9 to 37) deal with the establishment of free trade between members, and the erection of the Common Customs Tariff against the rest of the world. Britain would have to end the Imperial Preference given to Commonwealth countries, and, instead, would have to discriminate against them; also she must soon lose the Preference which she gets from them.   The major Preference givers are Australia, New Zealand, Canada and South Africa, who together bought about as much from Britain in 1965 as Common Market Six.

(12) PERMANENCE

Unlike every other major treaty-e.g. EFTA, GATT, the Test-Ban agreement-there is no provision for withdrawal.
The only relevant Article, is 240, reading-
"This Treaty is concluded for an unlimited period."
This unique provision means that once in, no member of his own sole free will has any legitimate treaty right to withdraw. In any event, as time passes, Britain would increasingly become more involved and so tied to EEC as to make withdrawal impossible.

The Rome Treaty contains no definite commitment to any further, precise political moves. However, all members accept the implication that some new, overall constitutional apparatus will evolve; it might be a federal United States of Europe or a looser confederal grouping, in both cases doubtless with a powerful politician at the top as President.

At present, if Britain ever signs the Treaty, the whole concept of rule in Britain by the "Queen in Parliament" is impaired. Under such, new form of European Constitution, the Queen and the British monarchy would stand inferior to a politically-motivated European president.

Joining the Common Market, one Labour MP, Desmond Donnelly, has said (27th November, 1965), "...could mean the end of the House of Lords with the Monarchy being declared redundant." He continued: "We could become part of a great new European State, probably governed by federal parliament and headed by elected President of Europa."

Before the Treaty of Rome is signed, the British voter surely has the right to have the matter fully explained to him and to be asked directly, whether by referendum, plebiscite or other means free of all other considerations, for his consent to step with such far-reaching consequences.

After the 2015 General Election - there will not be another opportunity to do anything else about the influx of immigrants coming into the UK, until 2020. And as proven in this book; apart from UKIP, all the other main political party's priorities are for the UK to remain in Europe.

It means absolutely nothing when MPs, such as the Prime Minister David Cameron's promise of a referendum, for he has no intention for his party to leave the EU.

Take note of what he really said on Wednesday 23 January 2013; "The next Conservative manifesto in 2015 will ask for a mandate from the British people for a Conservative government to 'negotiate a new settlement' with our European partners in the next Parliament." - "It will be a relationship with the single market at its heart.   And when we have 'negotiated that new settlement', we will give the British people a referendum with a very simple 'in or out' choice: to stay in the EU on these new terms or come out altogether." He said.

The deep-seated underlying factor of being a member of the EU, are that 'Articles 48 to 73 Free Movement of Labour' clauses within the "treaties" - cannot and never will be negotiated by the European Commission.

First published Monday 3 November 2014 in National News it states: 'Angela Merkel had made it clear, that Germany, like the UK, is concerned about the abuse of free movement to claim benefits, said Steffen Seibert a spokesman for Germany's government.

But added: "The general principle of freedom of movement in the European Union is not negotiable."

So here's the farce, for Cameron already knows what needs to be 'negotiated' - is non-negotiable. Overlooking one vital matter and the biggest concern of the British public; the matter of "immigration," anything else possibly negotiable isn't really too much of worry to them, - other than perhaps the astronomical costs involved.

It was under Labour's "open door" immigration policy, that more than 3.2million arrivals from overseas simply entered the country.

There is no way anyone concerned about immigration will ever trust them again in regards to this matter.

The other major problem is that those currently in power don't even seem to be acknowledging the overbearing costs that all this immigration is having on the public purse, thus not factoring-in the additional costs and requirements involved into their future calculations and forecasts.

According to a statement by Alp Mehmet, Vice Chairman of Migration Watch - on the 27 February 2015;

"The Department of Communities and Local Government has today published its household projections for England out to 2037 in which they state that future increases in households will come overwhelmingly from population growth, with an extra 5.2 million households by 2037; an increase of 4,000 households per week."

"About 85% of population growth since 2000 has been as a result of immigration. In the long run all population growth in the UK is projected to come from immigration. However, unlike previous household projections from the DCLG, there is no estimate of the magnitude of its role in household increase. Indeed, there is no mention of immigration at all in their report."

Migration Watch UK have pointed out six key facts about the impact of immigration;

• Net migration nearly quadrupled from 48,000 in 1997 to 185,000 in 2003. Once the East Europeans had been granted free movement in 2004 it peaked at 320,000 in the year ending June 2005. Net foreign migration between 1997 and 2010 totaled nearly 4 million, two thirds of it non EU.

•   In 2013 over half a million migrants arrived in Britain, more than the total population of Bradford. In the same year 314,000 migrants left so net migration was 212,000.

•   We must build a new home every seven minutes for new migrants for the next 20 years or so.

•   England (not the UK) is the second most crowded country in Europe, after the Netherlands, excluding island and city states.

•   The UK population is projected to grow by over 9 million (9.4m) in just 25 years' time, increasing from 64.7 million in 2013 to 73 million by 2039. Of this increase, about two thirds is projected to be due to future migrants and their children - the equivalent of the current populations of Birmingham, Leeds, Sheffield, Bradford, Manchester, Edinburgh, Liverpool, Bristol, Cardiff, Newcastle, Belfast and Aberdeen.

•   To keep the population of the UK below 70 million, net migration must be reduced to around 40,000 a year. It would then peak in mid-century at just under 70 million (about 69.7 million). Last revised July 2014.

We can't seem to better explain the impact and gravity of what continuous immigration will have on the future of the UK, than perhaps Lord Green of Deddington, Chairman of Migration Watch UK.

Whose own personal cautionary message - first published on the 1 March 2015, starkly expresses and forewarns of the pitfalls and outcome were his observations and words of advice to be ignored.

This is why the decision was made to end the book on his rather unsettling prognosis and poignant words of caution, that were anyone foolish enough to ignore these facts and interpretations from a worldwide expert on immigration; - then it's to their own peril.

They cannot complain and claim; "Why didn't anyone explain how serious this matter really was?"

"It is now 14 years since I co-founded Migrationwatch with Professor David Coleman of Oxford University. In the early years we had to face snide accusations of racism, notably from the BBC. Our aim was simply to get the facts about immigration properly understood and to have a sensible debate about the issues it raised.

We have now won that debate in the court of public opinion.

Poll after poll has shown that immigration is right up there with the economy as an issue of national concern. The polls also show that nearly 75 per cent wish to see a reduction in immigration, including 50 per cent who want to see it reduced 'by a lot'. This broad view is shared by members of the ethnic communities, among whom a majority wish to see a reduction.

Sadly, Thursday's immigration figures will have been a huge disappointment to the public. For the year ending last September, net migration reached nearly 300,000. This is three times the Government's target, and 50,000 higher than the level when the Government came to office.

Despite the clear and long-standing evidence of the strength of public opinion, some are today arguing that, instead of policies to reduce immigration, the objective should be to mitigate its impact. The clear implication, of course, is that since nothing can be done to control immigration, we might as well get used to it.

The public will simply not accept that position. They will be perfectly happy with controlled immigration at a sensible level.

They recognise its benefits in an open economy and society. The problem is one of scale and they realise that the implications of net migration on the present scale are breath-taking.

If this is allowed to continue, we will have to build the equivalent of three cities the size of Birmingham in the next five years. This is clearly impossible, so the effect will be even more overcrowding and congestion, particularly in our cities.

Worse, in just eight years the UK population would reach 70 million, and 80 million in 25 years and still climbing. The sooner we get a grip, the better.

Apart from the impossibility of building infrastructure on such a scale, our public services are coming under increasing strain. This has practical consequences. A neighbour of mine who was checking in to her local GP's surgery had to tap the screen to choose a language. The top option was not even English – it was Polish.

The metropolitan elite who are so keen on immigration may well have health insurance but, for those sitting in the queue, it is altogether different.

No less important is our social cohesion. We already face a situation in which immigrant children in our cities find themselves in schools with virtually no UK-born children. Indeed, net foreign migration since 1998 comes to a total of more than four million. How can we possibly achieve integration at such a pace?

We now face what might amount to a conspiracy of silence. The three main parties all have good reasons to avoid immigration during the coming Election campaign.

The Conservatives, despite genuine efforts and support from the top when it was needed, have not succeeded in getting the numbers down. Labour know that it was under their watch that immigration first spun out of control. In 1997, net migration was a mere 48,000. This trebled in a couple of years before reaching a peak of 320,000 in 2005.

They clearly had a deliberate policy of increasing immigration, but failed to mention it in their three manifestos during that period. Furthermore, the policies they are suggesting now will have no significant impact on numbers – an aspect which they decline even to discuss.

233

As for the Liberal Democrats, they have never believed in reducing immigration and, in Coalition government, they have done their best to hamper attempts to limit it.

Any such outcome would be reinforced by BBC home affairs editors and producers – many of whom are only too happy to avoid the subject, and especially any serious treatment of the case against mass immigration, whenever they can. This leaves the puzzle as to how immigration could have increased so rapidly in the face of the Government's commitments.

There were two main factors. Economic migrants from outside the EU increased significantly, and migrants from the EU itself doubled in the past two years.

The Government is trying to spin this as 'a problem of success.' The Treasury has long favoured high immigration because it gives the impression that the economy is growing that much faster.

However, what really matters is not the size of the economy but wealth per head. All the evidence is that the impact of immigration on this key measure is extremely small. Nor is there any benefit to the national budget.

If you choose a particular group of immigrants over a particular period, you can get a positive result, but even immigration enthusiasts have had to admit that the budgetary cost of all immigration since 1997 has been somewhere between £115 billion and £160 billion.

It cannot possibly be the case that, on a small island, we are really unable to control our borders. So what can be done?

There is no need for yet more laws. The present rules need to be implemented more effectively with close attention paid to each route of entry and, crucially, to departures.

The first step must be to restore exit checks as people leave Britain. Incredible though it may seem, these have not been in operation for 20 years. As a result, the Government has no idea whatsoever who is on this island. Exit controls, due at last to come into effect next May, will make a start on that.

For example, non-EU students are a major concern. Despite a barrage of propaganda from the education sector, the fact is that they have been arriving at the rate of about 150,000 a year, but only 50,000 a year are leaving.

Exit checks will tell us who has not left, but those who overstay still have to be located and removed – a huge task which is pathetically under-resourced.

Fewer than 5,000 immigration offenders are being removed every year compared to an illegal immigrant population that could well be as many as one million.

A major increase in resources is therefore needed. At present only one quarter of one per cent of Government expenditure goes to immigration control. We have called for this to be doubled. Serious issues call for serious funds. As for EU migrants, we have the promise of a negotiation to reduce their access to benefits. It remains to be seen whether this will have much effect.

There may well have to be a much tougher negotiation with our partners. In the meantime, UKIP must have been smiling all the way to their spring conference. Unfortunately, their prospects of ensuring any effective action are very slim.

Nevertheless, they will certainly gain from a public mood of disillusionment, amounting to anger, at the failure of successive governments to heed their views on immigration. Continued failure to respond to overwhelming public concern carries a risk to confidence in our political system as a whole." - Lord Green of Deddington, Chairman of Migration Watch UK 1 March 2015.

"IMMIGRATION, IMMIGRATION, IMMIGRATION!"

Sources:http://www.bbc.co.uk/history/british/modern/windrush_01.shtml
http://forums.ozreggae.com/index.php?showtopic=620
http://www.bnvillage.co.uk/black-roots-village/71045-windrush-era-print.html
http://en.wikipedia.org/wiki?curid=30032561

MATH – NOT RACISM

Sources:
http://www.greenfieldreporter.com/view/story/d76e713a0c214eb0b1dc8c0f21486671/EU--Serbia-Migrants-Germanyhttp://article.wn.com/view/2015/02/13/Hungary_to_legislate_for_detention_or_rapid_deportation_of_m_4/
http://www.bbc.co.uk/news/uk-31519319
http://www.independent.co.uk/news/uk/home-news/more-than-1700-people-apply-for-just-eight-jobs-at-costa-coffee-shop-8501329.html
http://www.huffingtonpost.co.uk/2014/03/24/aldi-1500jobs-unemployment_n_5020212.html

DELIBERATE DECEPTION
ACT OF TREASON

Sources:
http://bloginfo.educate-yourself.eu/2012/12/the-nazi-roots-of-the-brussels-eu-update/
http://www.worldcoal.com/coal/17102013/The_mining_landscape_Part_One_140/
http://www.telegraph.co.uk/news/politics/conservative/10597409/Home-Office-hid-dossier-on-EU-migrants.html
http://www.telegraph.co.uk/news/uknews/immigration/8339075/More-than-three-million-migrants-under-Labour.html
http://www.express.co.uk/news/history/464014/Vikings-live-on-1million-Britons-alive-today-are-direct-descendants-of-the-Vikings
http://www.telegraph.co.uk/news/uknews/immigration/8339075/More-than-three-million-migrants-under-Labour.html
http://www.telegraph.co.uk/news/uknews/immigration/6762299/Record-level-of-British-population-is-foreign-born.html
http://www.princeton.edu/~achaney/tmve/wiki100k/docs/Treason.html
http://www.londonlovesbusiness.com/business-news/politics/mandelson-labour-sent-search-parties-to-get-immigrants-to-come-to-uk/5495.article

http://www.dailymail.co.uk/news/article-2324112/Lord-Mandelson-Immigrants-We-sent-search-parties-hard-Britons-work.html
http://www.standard.co.uk/news/uk/800000-uk-jobs-advertised-across-europe--and-foreign-jobseekers-even-get-travelling-costs-8734731.html

NANNYGATE

Sources:
http://www.telegraph.co.uk/news/uknews/immigration/10684827/Nannygate-immigration-and-why-the-Tories-are-at-war.html
http://immigrationmatters.co.uk/2014/03
http://www.workpermit.com/news/2014-03-19/uk-pm-caught-up-in-immigration-row
http://www.bbc.co.uk/news/uk-politics-29358552
http://blogs.telegraph.co.uk/news/jameskirkup/100262397/immigration-shock-you-dear-reader-are-a-member-of-the-wealthy-metropolitan-elite/

LIES, DAMNED LIES & STATISTICS

Source: http://www.bbc.co.uk/news/uk-31519319

FOOD POVERTY IN THE UK

Sources:
http://nhsfightback.org/2015/01/14/millions-in-britain-cannot-afford-to-eat-properly/
http://www.wsws.org/en/articles/2015/01/12/food-j12.html

"LEGAL" & "UNAUTHORISED"

Sources:
https://www.youtube.com/watch?v=e7J-RU_R5nQ
http://en.wikipedia.org/wiki/Illegal_immigration_in_the_United_Kingdom
http://edition.pagesuite-professional.co.uk/Launch.aspx?PBID=2e06ba4c-0895-4d35-96f7-203988cdd8b9
http://article.wn.com/view/2014/11/28/Immigration_David_Cameron_to_outline_benefit_restrictions/
http://article.wn.com/view/2015/03/03/Act_now_to_overhaul_Britains_shocking_detention_of_migrants_/
http://www.dailymail.co.uk/news/article-2379478/Revealed-How-500-000-immigrants-given-social-housing-decade-number-families-waiting-list-hits-record-high.html
http://en.wikipedia.org/wiki/Illegal_immigration_in_the_United_Kingdom
http://www.ilfordrecorder.co.uk/news/rich_boroughs_buy_up_cheap_homes_1_3961818

FREE MOVEMENT OF LABOUR

Sources:
http://www.thaivisa-express.com/schengen-visa/
http://ec.europa.eu/dgs/home-affairs/what-we-do/policies/borders-and-visas/schengen-information-system/index_en.htm
https://www.gov.uk/living-in-switzerland
https://www.youtube.com/watch?v=LkIC4_Jjn60
http://www.telegraph.co.uk/news/politics/conservative/10597409/Home-Office-hid-dossier-on-EU-migrants.html

THE MEDIA'S PRO-IMMIGRATION AGENDA
IMMIGRATION CENTRES
BBC EU FUNDING - Ukips
TROJAN HORSES

Sources:
http://blogs.spectator.co.uk/culturehousedaily/2014/02/the-millions-in-eu-funding-the-bbc-tried-to-hide/
Sources:
http://www.channel4.com/programmes/ukip-the-first-100-days
http://article.wn.com/view/2014/10/19/Barroso_warns_Cameron_that_arbitrary_migration_cap_would_bre/
http://news.sky.com/story/1126564/probe-into-governments-go-home-poster-van
http://en.wikipedia.org/wiki/Illegal_immigration_in_the_United_Kingdom
http://www.bbc.co.uk/comedy/tilldeathusdopart/
http://www.channel4.com/programmes/the-romanians-are-coming
http://www.dailymail.co.uk/news/article-2968086/Makers-Immigration-Street-documentary-accused-hindering-police-probe-alleged-crimes-committed-filming.html
http://www.channel4.com/programmes/benefits-street
https://www.youtube.com/watch?v=nYcQyFiJaaQ
http://en.wikipedia.org/wiki/List_of_QI_episodes
http://www.comedy.co.uk/guide/tv/russell_howards_good_news/videos/5458/ukips_perfect_candidate/
http://en.wikipedia.org/wiki/Winston_McKenzie
http://www.theguardian.com/politics/2013/aug/07/godfrey-bloom-regret-bongo-land-ukip
http://www.politics.co.uk/news/2013/09/20/nigel-farage-schoolboy-fascist
http://news.sky.com/story/1398790/ukips-first-mp-warns-party-against-racism
http://www.theguardian.com/politics/2014/apr/24/ukip-member-broadcast-

suspended-racist-tweets
http://www.bbc.co.uk/news/uk-politics-31565770
http://politicalscrapbook.net/2012/09/golliwog-baiting-former-tory-to-stand-for-ukip-in-police-elections/
http://en.wikipedia.org/wiki/World_War_II_casualties

A VIRTUOUS CONCEPTION
EUROSCEPTICS

Sources:
http://www.worldometers.info/world-population/
http://www.bbc.co.uk/news/business-30875633
http://en.wikipedia.org/wiki/Get_Britain_Out
http://en.wikipedia.org/wiki/Campaign_for_an_Independent_Britain
http://campaignforanindependentbritain.org.uk/
http://civitas.org.uk/newblog/tag/anti-federalist-league/
http://en.wikipedia.org/wiki/Referendum_Party
http://geography.about.com/od/politicalgeography/a/turkeyeu.htm

EU - REFERENDUMS
FINANCIAL SINKHOLES
TROIKA

Sources:
http://news.bbc.co.uk/onthisday/hi/dates/stories/january/1/newsid_2459000/2459167.stm
http://www.bbc.co.uk/news/uk-politics-15390884
http://www.mediander.com/connects/19826/michael-foot/#!/980599/peter-shore
http://en.wikipedia.org/wiki/United_Kingdom_European_Communities_membership_referendum,_1975
http://www.huffingtonpost.co.uk/2014/02/24/child-poverty-ids_n_4846974.html
http://www.telegraph.co.uk/finance/economics/9410648/Britains-main-export-market-is-no-longer-the-EU.html
http://www.government-online.net/cameron-eu-referendum-2017/
http://www.independent.co.uk/news/uk/politics/ukip-timeline-the-gradual-rise-to-westminster-9874423.html
http://www.ukip.org/splash2?splash=1
http://newseurope.me/2015/01/06/iceland-withdraw-eu-application-prime-minister/
http://en.wikipedia.org/wiki/National_Front_(UK)
Sources:
http://en.wikipedia.org/wiki/Purchasing_power_parity

http://www.telegraph.co.uk/news/worldnews/europe/eu/9628535/EU-demands-an-extra-11.5bn-from-British-taxpayers.html
http://www.cco.net/~trufax/stories/banking2012-2.html
http://www.telegraph.co.uk/news/worldnews/europe/greece/
Source: https://www.imf.org/external/np/exr/facts/europe.htm

"WAG THE DOG" – WAR
NATO's – EUROPEAN ARMY

Sources: http://en.wikipedia.org/wiki/History_of_Ukraine
http://en.wikipedia.org/wiki/Euromaidan
Rajan Menon (28 January 2014). "Ukraine: Is Yanukovych Finished?". The National Interest. p. 3. Retrieved 30 January 2014.
Kathy Lally (11 March 2014). "Ousted Ukraine president warns of civil war, criticizes U.S. for aiding current government". The Washington Post. Washington Post. Retrieved 17 March 2014.
Maxim Eristavi (2 March 2014). "How Ukraine's Parliament Brought Down Yanukovych". The Daily Beast. Retrieved 17 March 2014.
"Berkut Riot Police Used to Falsify Ukrainian Parliamentary Elections", The Jamestown Foundation (14 November 2012)
"Ukraine Violence Leaves at Least 10 Dead". ABC News. 18 February 2014. Archived from the original on 22 February 2014. Retrieved 18 February 2014.
"Ukraine: Speaker Oleksandr Turchynov named interim president", BBC News (23 February 2014)
"Ukraine protests timeline", BBC News (23 February 2014)
"Ukraine bloodshed: Kiev death toll jumps to 77 — RT News". Rt.com. Retrieved 2014-02-25.
"Ukraine crisis: deal signed in effort to end Kiev standoff". The Guardian. 21 February 2014.
Ukrainian ex-leader Viktor Yanukovych vows fightback, BBC News (28 February 2014
"Archrival Is Freed as Ukraine Leader Flees". The New York Times. 22 February 2014. Retrieved 23 February 2014.
b John Feffer. "Who Are These 'People,' Anyway? | John Feffer". Huffingtonpost.com. Retrieved 2014-03-17.
c"Rada removes Yanukovych from office, schedules new elections for May 25", Interfax-Ukraine (24 February 2014)
Sindelar, Daisy (23 February 2014). "Was Yanukovych's Ouster Constitutional?". Radio Free Europe, Radio Liberty (Rferl.org). Retrieved 25 February 2014.
David Stern (2014-02-22). "BBC News - Ukrainian MPs vote to oust President Yanukovych". Bbc.co.uk. Retrieved 2014-03-17.
b"Постанова про усунення і результати голосування по ній на сайті верховної ради України" (Ukrainian)

241

b"Рада усунула Януковича - на сайті Української правди"
b"warrant out for Viktor Yanukovych's arrest, says interior minister".
Guardian. 24 February 2014. Retrieved 24 February 2014.
Fromkin, David. Europe's last summer: who started the Great War in 1914?.
New York : Knopf : 2004. pp. 88–92. ISBN 978-0-375-41156-4.
The Kaiser and His Court: Wilhelm II and the Government of Germany by John
C. G. Röhl; Translated by Terence F. Cole, Cambridge University Press; 288
pages. p. 257.
Röhl, John C G. 1914: Delusion or Design. Elek. pp. 29–32. ISBN 0-236-15466-4.
http://www.bbc.co.uk/news/world-europe-31669061
http://www.trumanlibrary.org/oralhist/achilles.htm
http://www.bbc.co.uk/news/world-europe-31796337

DON'T MENTION ZEE VAR

Sources: Zalampas, Michael (1989). Adolf Hitler and the Third Reich in
American magazines, 1923–1939. Bowling Green University Popular Press.
ISBN 0-87972-462-5.
Taylor, Jay (2009). The Generalissimo: Chiang Kai-shek and the Struggle for
Modern China. Cambridge, MA: Harvard University Press. ISBN 978-0-674-
03338-2.
"Khalkhin-Gol: The Forgotten War" (1983).
http://en.wikipedia.org/wiki/World_War_I
http://en.wikipedia.org/wiki/World_War_II
http://www.reject-the-eu.co.uk/

WWII

http://en.wikipedia.org/wiki/World_War_II#CITEREFKantowicz1999
Kantowicz 1999, p. 149
Davies 2008, pp. 134–140.
Shaw 2000, p. 35.
Bullock 1990, p. 265.
Preston 1998, p. 104.
Myers & Peattie 1987, p. 458.
Smith & Steadman 2004, p. 28.
Coogan 1993: "Although some Chinese troops in the Northeast managed to
retreat south, others were trapped by the advancing Japanese Army and were
faced with the choice of resistance in defiance of orders, or surrender. A few
commanders submitted, receiving high office in the puppet government, but
others took up arms against the invader. The forces they commanded were
the first of the volunteer armies."
Brody 1999, p. 4.
Dawood & Mitra 2012.
Zalampas 1989, p. 62.
Mandelbaum 1988, p. 96; Record 2005, p. 50.

Schmitz 2000, p. 124.
Andrea L. Stanton, Edward Ramsamy, Peter J. Seybolt. Cultural Sociology of the Middle East, Asia, and Africa: An Encyclopedia. p. 308. Retrieved 2014-04-06.
Kitson 2001, p. 231.
Adamthwaite 1992, p. 52.
Graham 2005, p. 110.
Busky 2002, p. 10.

THE NAZI ROOTS OF THE BRUSSELS EU
THE GREATER SPHERE CARTEL

Source: http://www.reject-the-eu.co.uk/
Source: www.profit-over-life.org
Source: www.cartel-roots-ww2.org
http://www.relay-of-life.org/nazi-roots/pdf/chap-uk-hallstein.pdf
http://www4.dr-rath-foundation.org/open_letters/soelter.html

THE TREATIES

Source:
http://www.europeanlawmonitor.org/treaties/eu-treaties-treaty-on-european-union-maastricht-treaty-of-nice-lisbon-treaty.html

JOINING THE COMMON MARKET – 1967

Source: Joining the Common Market or What the Treaty of Rome Means - Political Intelligence Publications Ltd. - "Immigration, immigration, immigration!"

UK POPULATION TO HIT 80 MILLION IF...

Source: http://migrationwatch.com/

www.ingramcontent.com/pod-product-compliance
Lightning Source LLC
Chambersburg PA
CBHW070637290526
45790CB00001B/121